Better Homes and Gardens®

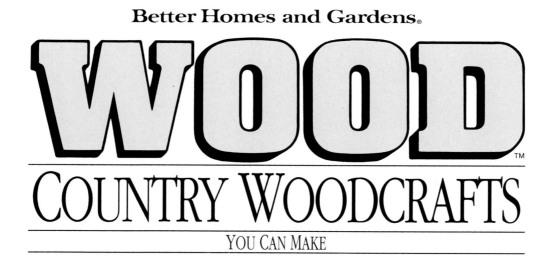

# WOOD™
## COUNTRY WOODCRAFTS
### YOU CAN MAKE

All of us at Meredith® Books are dedicated to giving you the
information and ideas you need to create beautiful and useful
woodworking projects. We guarantee your satisfaction with this
book for as long as you own it. We also welcome your comments
and suggestions. Please write us at Meredith® Books, BB-117,
1100 Walnut St., Des Moines, IA 50309-3400.

A **WOOD**™ **BOOK**
Published by Meredith® Books

**MEREDITH® BOOKS**
President, Book Group: Joseph J. Ward
Vice President and Editorial Director: Elizabeth P. Rice
Executive Editor: Connie Schrader
Art Director: Ernest Shelton
Prepress Production Manager: Randall Yontz

WOOD® MAGAZINE
President, Magazine Group: William T. Kerr
Editor: Larry Clayton

**COUNTRY WOODCRAFTS YOU CAN MAKE**
**Produced by Roundtable Press, Inc.**
Directors: Susan E. Meyer, Marsha Melnick
Senior Editor: Sue Heinemann
Managing Editor: Ross L. Horowitz
Graphic Designer: Leah Lococo
Art Assistant: Ahmad Mallah
Copy Assistant: Amy Handy

**For Meredith® Books**
Assistant Art Director: Tom Wegner
Contributing How-To Editor: Marlen Kemmet
Contributing Tool Editor: Larry Johnston
Contributing Outline Editor: David A. Kirchner

Special thanks to Khristy Benoit and Kathy Stevens

On the front cover: Shaker Oval Carrier, pages 44–47
On the back cover (clockwise from top left):
    Odds 'N' Ends Country Shadow Box, pages 48–50;
    Colonial Candle Box, pages 58–61; Early-American
    Candlestand, pages 62–64; Pilgrim's-Pride Wall Box,
    page 65; Country Clock, pages 66–67; Early-Days Sofa
    Table, pages 88–92; Kitchen Canisters, pages 12–14

# FOR THE HEART OF THE HOME

*You can give a real sense of country in your kitchen by introducing homey accents in unexpected places. Here are nine projects that will add a touch of Americana to the everyday activities around mealtimes.*

# COUNTRY-KITCHEN
# BUTTER CHURN

**K**itty knows a good project when she sees one. Our full-sized pine butter churn may be just the right country accent your home needs. We provide jigs for cutting the tapered barrel pieces, a jig for routing the circular lid and bottom, and the pattern for the stencil that adorns the churn's front.

### First, cut the tapered barrel staves

**1.** From ¾"-thick pine stock, rip and crosscut 16—2x20½" barrel staves (A). (See the Cutting Diagram.) Next, angle your tablesaw blade 4° from center. (We set the blade angle with an adjustable triangle.) Select the best side of each stave for the outside face and mark it. Now, strike a square line across the good face ½" up from one end of each stave. Now, bevel-crosscut each stave along that line so that the outside face on each measures 20" long.

**2.** From ¾"-thick plywood or particleboard, make the two taper jigs using the dimensions shown on the Taper Jig drawing. (We made the jigs from two pieces measuring 5½x24" by first setting the tablesaw blade to cut an 11° bevel, the fence 5" from the blade, and then bevel-ripping one edge on both pieces. Next, we laid out the notches on the jig blanks, and then cut them to shape with a portable jigsaw.) Cut the notches carefully so the staves fit snugly in the jig. Nail cleats across the corners of the jigs where shown (we used scrap ¼"-thick plywood). Number the jigs 1 and 2.

**3.** With your tablesaw blade still angled at 11°, place jig 1 on the saw table with the beveled edge against the saw blade. (Our tablesaw blade tilts to the *continued*

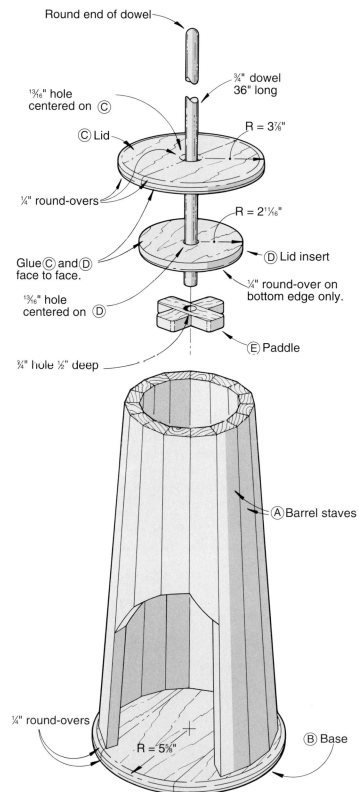

Round end of dowel

¾" dowel 36" long

¹³⁄₁₆" hole centered on Ⓒ

R = 3⅞"

Ⓒ Lid

¼" round-overs

R = 2¹¹⁄₁₆"

Ⓓ Lid insert

Glue Ⓒ and Ⓓ face to face.

¹³⁄₁₆" hole centered on Ⓓ

¼" round-over on bottom edge only.

Ⓔ Paddle

¾" hole ½" deep

Ⓐ Barrel staves

¼" round-overs

R = 5⅝"

Ⓑ Base

# COUNTRY-KITCHEN BUTTER CHURN
*continued*

right and we positioned the fence to the right of it.) Lock the fence against the jig. Now, position the jig so it clears the blade and insert a stave outside facedown in the jig's notch, and rip the first tapered bevel as shown *below*. Cut the other 15 staves.

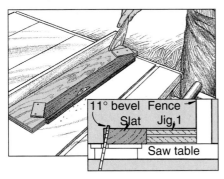

11° bevel  Fence
Slat  Jig 1
Saw table

**4.** Without changing the saw setting, place jig 2 on the saw table with the beveled edge against the saw blade. Next, insert a stave in the jig outside facedown and the square edge out. Rip the second tapered bevel using the same procedure. Make the identical saw cut on the remaining 15 staves.

**Next, glue-assemble the barrel**

**Note:** *To save glue cleanup work later, adhere strips of masking tape along both edges on the face of each tapered stave.*

**1.** To form the churn's barrel (see the Exploded View drawing on page 5), apply glue (we used white woodworker's glue) to the beveled edges of each stave. (As shown *above*, we arranged the glued staves inside a two-gallon paint pail.) Finish aligning all of the glued staves into a circle in the barrel. Place a web clamp around the middle of the assembly to draw it together. Remove the assembly from the pail, check stave alignment around the outside and for level on the bottom. Next, place web clamps around the

barrel near the top and the bottom, as shown *above*. Wipe off any glue squeeze-out. Set the barrel aside until the glue dries.

**2.** For the churn's base (B), the lid (C), and the lid insert (D), make up one 12" square, one 9" square, and one 6" square of ¾"-thick pine. (We edge-joined 2" widths of boards to minimize the chance of warpage.) Draw diagonals from corner to corner on the underside of each square and mark the centerpoints. Next, drive a 4d finish nail ½" deep into the centerpoint of each square to use as the pivot point for the router's trammel base. Now, cut off the nails, leaving about ½" exposed above the surface of the wood.

**3.** Make a trammel base to fit your router, using the dimensions on the Trammel Base Drawing on page 7. Now, remove the regular base from your router and mount the trammel base to your router.

**4.** Clamp a large piece of scrap to the top of your bench or work area. Next, one by one place the squares on the scrap and drive two 2d finish nails through opposite corners to hold them firmly in place. Now, using your router, the trammel base, and a ¼"-straight router bit, cut the base, lid, and lid insert to shape, as shown *below*. Use pivot hole A on the trammel to cut the base,

hole B for the lid, and hole C to cut the lid insert. (We set the router to cut in ¼" deep initially, and then lowered the bit in ¼" increments.)

**5.** Remove the nails from the discs. Rout ¼" round-overs along the edges of each, where shown on the Exploded View drawing. Drill a 13/16" hole through the center of the lid and the lid insert. (We used a spade bit, or you can sand the inside of a ¾" hole.) Glue the lid insert to the underside of the lid.

**6.** Form the paddle (E) as shown on the drawing on page 8. (Beginning with a 12"-long piece, we first cut two 1"-wide dadoes ⅜" deep starting 1¼" from each end, using a tablesaw. Then, we trimmed the pieces to length, and rounded the corners.) Glue the two E's together to form a cross. Next, drill a ¾"-diameter hole, ½" deep into the center of the paddle. Sand
*continued*

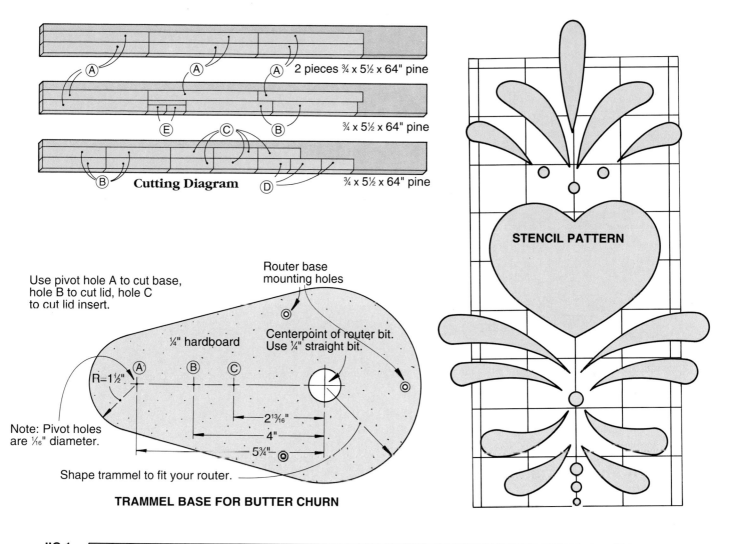

**Cutting Diagram**

2 pieces ¾ x 5½ x 64" pine

¾ x 5½ x 64" pine

¾ x 5½ x 64" pine

Use pivot hole A to cut base, hole B to cut lid, hole C to cut lid insert.

Router base mounting holes

¼" hardboard

Centerpoint of router bit. Use ¼" straight bit.

R=1½"

Note: Pivot holes are 1⁄16" diameter.

2¹³⁄₁₆"

4"

5¾"

Shape trammel to fit your router.

**TRAMMEL BASE FOR BUTTER CHURN**

**STENCIL PATTERN**

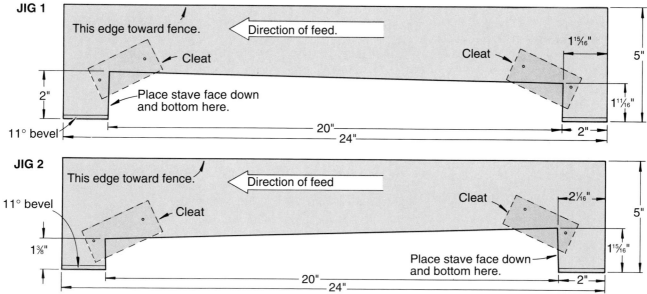

**JIG 1**

This edge toward fence.

Direction of feed.

Cleat

Cleat

1¹⁵⁄₁₆"

5"

2"

Place stave face down and bottom here.

1¹¹⁄₁₆"

11° bevel

20"

24"

2"

**JIG 2**

This edge toward fence.

Direction of feed

Cleat

Cleat

2¹⁄₁₆"

5"

11° bevel

1⅜"

Place stave face down and bottom here.

1¹⁵⁄₁₆"

20"

24"

2"

# COUNTRY-KITCHEN
# BUTTER CHURN
*continued*

one end of a 36" long ¾" dowel round. Now, glue the flat end in the hole in the paddle.

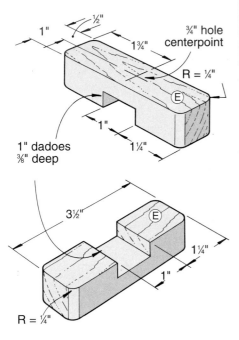

1"
½"
1¾"
¾" hole centerpoint
R = ¼"
E
1"
1"
1¼"
1" dadoes ⅜" deep

3½"
E
1¼"
1"
R = ¼"

### Bill of Materials

| Part | Finished Size* | | | Mat. | Qty. |
|------|------|------|------|------|------|
| | T | W | L | | |
| A* | ¾" | 2" | 20" | pine | 16 |
| B* | ¾" | 11¼" dia. | | pine | 1 |
| C* | ¾" | 7¾" dia. | | pine | 1 |
| D* | ¾" | 5⅜" dia. | | pine | 1 |
| E* | ¾" | 1" | 3½" | pine | 2 |

*Parts marked with an * are cut larger initially, and then trimmed to finished size. Please read the instructions before cutting.

**Supplies:** 1—¾ x 36" dowel, ¾" plywood or particleboard, stencil Mylar, finish.

## The final assembly and finishing

**1.** Remove the web clamps and the masking tape from the barrel staves. Scrape off any remaining glue squeeze-out. Finish-sand the barrel and the other parts, sanding with the grain. (We used 180- and 220-grit sandpaper, sanding just enough to remove the sharp edges.)

**2.** Test-fit the barrel on the base. Next, center the barrel on the base and place several pencil marks around it to aid repositioning. Liberally apply glue to the bottom of the barrel, and place it on the base. Wipe off glue squeeze-out, and weight the barrel down until the glue dries.

**3.** Apply the finish of your choice. (We stained the barrel, paddle, and paddle handle; we painted the base and lid, masking the bottom of the barrel with tape to avoid getting paint on it.)

**4.** Transfer the stencil pattern on page 7 to an 11x17" sheet of stenciling Mylar (available at crafts supply stores). Cut out the design with a crafts knife. Paint the decorative stencil on the barrel in the colors of your choice. (We positioned our stencil 2½" from the top edge.)

### Project Tool List
Tablesaw
Portable jigsaw
Router
   ¼" straight bit
   ¼" round-over bit
Drill
Bits: 1/16", 3/16", ¾", 13/16"
Web clamps
Finishing sander

***Note:*** *We built this project using the tools listed. You may be able to substitute other tools and equipment for listed items you don't have. You'll also need various common hand tools and clamps to complete the project.*

# OAK BREAKFAST TRAY

You can also use this classic serving tray for supper by the TV, appetizers at a party, or desserts on the patio. Box joints and durable oak team up to make this project as tough as it is eye-pleasing.

**Note:** *You'll need some ½" oak for this project. You can resaw your own, or order.*

### Building the jig
**1.** Build the box-joint jig by first cutting the plywood to size for the fence, and the pine for the stop block to the dimensions shown in the Box-Joint Jig drawing. Glue and clamp the two pine pieces to make the stop block shown in the drawing at right.
**2.** Unplug your table saw. Remove the table insert and trace its outline on a piece of ¼" hardboard. (Some saws require a thicker insert; simply plane thicker stock if yours does. The top of the insert should sit flush with the surface of the saw table.) Cut and

sand the edges until the insert fits snugly in the recess.
**3.** Mount a dado blade or dado-blade set to your tablesaw, and set it to cut ¼" wide. Position the insert in the sawtable recess, and clamp a piece of scrap 2×4 across, but not directly over, the center of the insert. Plug the saw in and start the

motor. Raise the rotating blade so that it cuts through the insert to a cutting height of ⅝". Turn the saw off, and lower the blade back to a cutting height of ⅜". Remove the 2×4.
**4.** Clamp the jig fence securely to the miter gauge and square the miter gauge and jig fence with the dado blade. Run the jig fence across the dado blade to cut the first kerf. Remove the jig fence from the miter gauge, measure over *exactly* ¼", and mark the position of the second kerf, where shown in the Box-Joint Jig drawing. (If your dado cuts a fraction narrower or wider than ¼", adjust the size of the gap accordingly.)
**5.** Refasten the jig fence to the miter gauge. Raise the blade to ½" above the surface of the saw table, and cut the second kerf exactly where marked. Cut the guide pin to size and glue it in the first kerf. Remove any excess glue.

### Cutting the box joints
**1.** Rip and crosscut the two tray sides (A) to 2¼×24" and the two tray ends (B) to 3¹³⁄₁₆×12" from ½" oak stock. (The extra width allows for final trimming later.)  *continued*

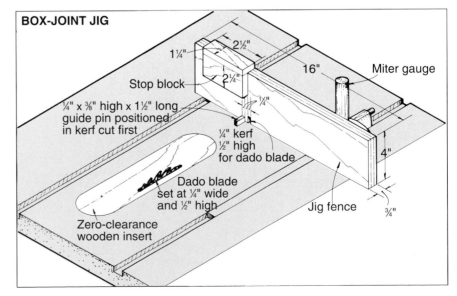

**BOX-JOINT JIG**

2½"

1¼"

2¼"

Stop block

16"

Miter gauge

¼" x ⅜" high x 1½" long guide pin positioned in kerf cut first

¼"

¼" kerf ½" high for dado blade

4"

Zero-clearance wooden insert

Dado blade set at ¼" wide and ½" high

Jig fence

¾"

# OAK BREAKFAST TRAY
*continued*

***Note:*** *Test-cut box joints in scrap material the same thickness as the tray sides and ends before you cut the ends of A and B.*

**2.** To cut the first notch, clamp one of the tray sides (A) to the box-joint jig with the left edge of A perfectly in line with the left edge of the kerf, as shown in the Step 1 drawing, *below left* (We used a stop block as shown to ensure that the edge of the side piece remained square with the saw table when we made the first cut.) Clamp the stop in position, clamp A to the jig, and cut where shown in the drawing. (When clamping A to the jig, make A sit flush on the saw table, not the insert. This will ensure that the notches will all be cut the same depth.)

**3.** Reposition A and the stop block so that the notch rests on the guide pin, as shown in the Step 2 drawing. Make the second cut. Continue to reposition part A and the stop block, making the cuts as shown in photo A, *above right*.

**4.** Flip A end over end, and cut the notches. Keep the edge that

will eventually be the bottom edge of the tray against the stop block when cutting the opposite end. This way, you wind up with a notch on the bottom edge of each end where shown in the Step 2 drawing. Cut the box joints on the ends of the second A.

**5.** To make the first finger, position B tightly against the guide pin where shown in the Step 3 drawing. Clamp the stop block in position and make the first cut.

**6.** Reposition B and the stop block so that the notch sits on the guide pin where shown in the Step 4 drawing. Make the second cut, and continue repositioning and cutting. Flip the piece end over end and cut the other end of each B, taking care to keep the bottom edge of B against the stop block.

## Assembling the tray

**1.** Using double-faced tape, attach the two end pieces (B) together, keeping the bottom and side edges flush. Lay out and mark

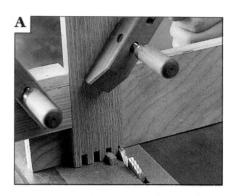

the handle shape and opening on one, where shown in the End View drawing.

**2.** Using a band saw or jigsaw, cut slightly outside the handle outline. Mount a 2½" sanding drum in a drill press. Attach a fence and a stop block to your drill-press table as shown in photo B. Sand the concave edges smooth, being careful not to burn the wood. (The fence and stop block help keep the sanding uniform on all radii.) You can also use the front roller on a belt sander to sand the radii smooth.

**3.** Use a drill press with a 1" bit to drill a hole at each end of the handle slot, backing the handle with scrap to prevent chip-out. Use a jigsaw or scroll saw to remove the stock left between the two holes. Sand the inside edges of the slots smooth.

**4.** Separate the two end pieces and scrape off any tape residue. Using a ⅛" round-over bit rout both inside edges of the handle slots. (If you don't have a ⅛" round-over bit, hand-sand a slight round-over.)

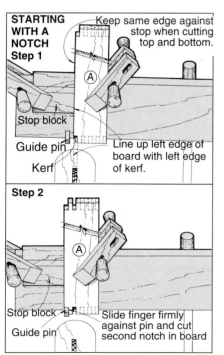

**STARTING WITH A NOTCH**
**Step 1**

Keep same edge against stop when cutting top and bottom.

(A)

Stop block

Guide pin

Kerf

Line up left edge of board with left edge of kerf.

**Step 2**

(A)

Stop block

Guide pin

Slide finger firmly against pin and cut second notch in board

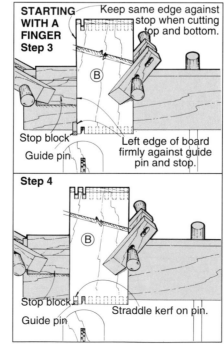

**STARTING WITH A FINGER**
**Step 3**

Keep same edge against stop when cutting top and bottom.

(B)

Stop block

Guide pin

Left edge of board firmly against guide pin and stop.

**Step 4**

(B)

Stop block

Guide pin

Straddle kerf on pin.

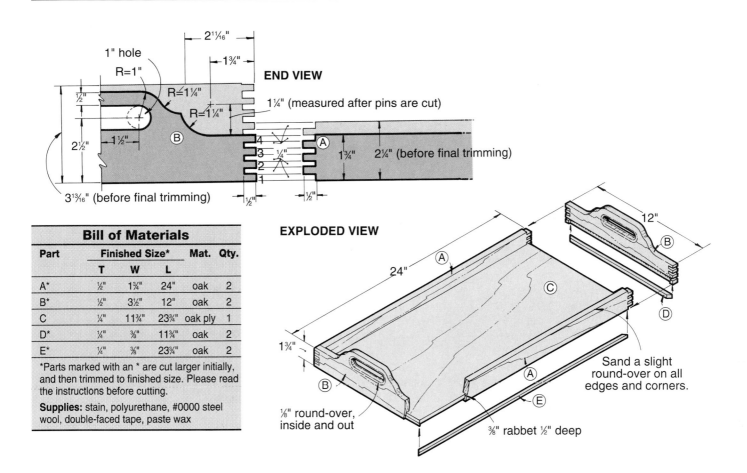

END VIEW

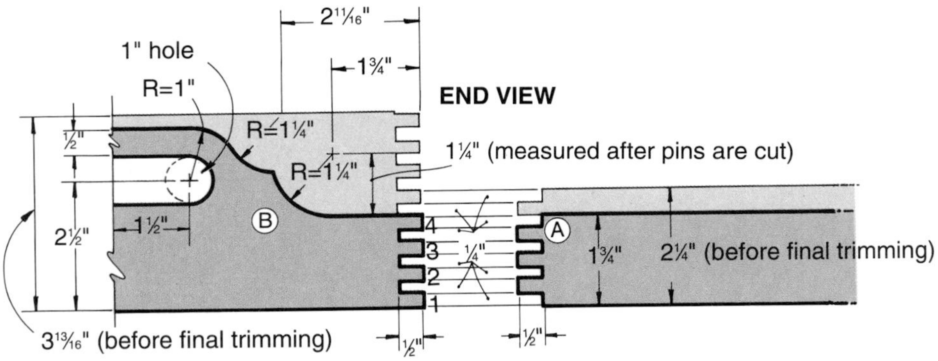
2¹¹⁄₁₆"
1" hole
R=1"
1¾"
R=1¼"
R=1¼"
½"
2½"
1½"
B
1¼" (measured after pins are cut)
A
4
3
2
1
¼"
1¾"
2¼" (before final trimming)
3¹³⁄₁₆" (before final trimming)
½"
½"

| Bill of Materials | | | | | |
|---|---|---|---|---|---|
| Part | Finished Size* | | | Mat. | Qty. |
| | T | W | L | | |
| A* | ½" | 1¾" | 24" | oak | 2 |
| B* | ½" | 3½" | 12" | oak | 2 |
| C | ¼" | 11¾" | 23¾" | oak ply | 1 |
| D* | ¼" | ⅜" | 11¾" | oak | 2 |
| E* | ¼" | ⅜" | 23¾" | oak | 2 |

*Parts marked with an * are cut larger initially, and then trimmed to finished size. Please read the instructions before cutting.

**Supplies:** stain, polyurethane, #0000 steel wool, double-faced tape, paste wax

EXPLODED VIEW

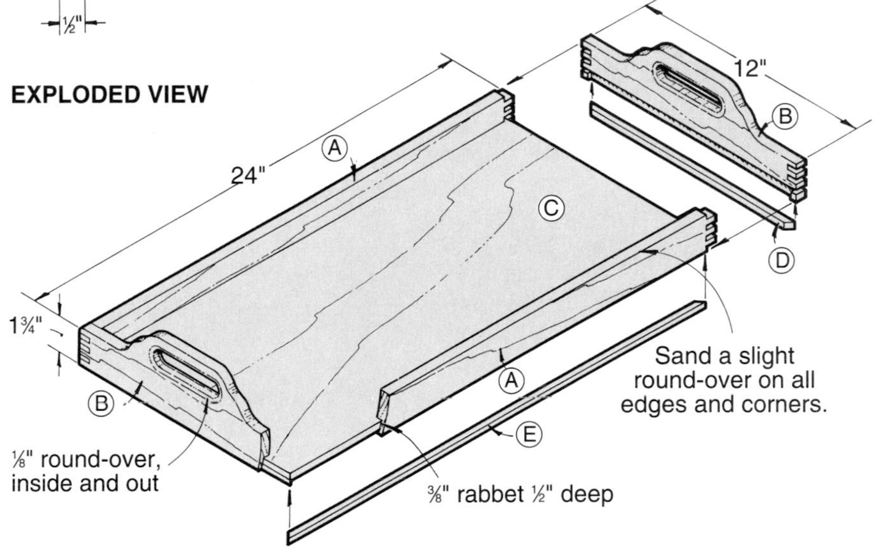
12"
B
24"
A
C
D
1¾"
Sand a slight round-over on all edges and corners.
A
B
E
⅛" round-over, inside and out
⅜" rabbet ½" deep

**Final steps before serving**

**1.** Dry-fit the ends and sides together, and mark the finished width on the top edge of the sides against the finished shape of the ends. Disassemble the pieces then rip the sides to width according to your marks. Sand the parts smooth.

**2.** Glue and clamp the sides and ends together, checking for square. Use a damp rag to remove glue squeeze-out from the inside of the corners. To ensure that the tray will sit flat, place waxed paper under the glued box joints, and clamp the tray frame to a flat surface. (We used a small brush to "paint" the glue into the notches. Then we clamped the tray frame to our saw table to keep the frame perfectly flat as the glue dried.)

**3.** Rout a ⅜" rabbet ½" deep along the inside of the bottom edge of the tray using a router with a ⅜" rabbeting bit. (We made two passes using a table-mounted router, raising the bit for the second pass to achieve the ½" depth needed.) Use a sharp chisel to square out the rabbets in each of the four corners.

**4.** Cut the bottom panel (C) to size from ¼" oak plywood. Check the fit of the panel in the rabbet in the tray frame and trim if necessary.

**5.** From ¾" oak stock, rip enough ¼"x⅜" strips to yield the bottom panel stops (D, E). Miter-cut the panel stops to finished length. With the bottom panel in place, glue and clamp the stops in place. Wipe off glue squeeze-out with a damp rag.

**6.** When the glue dries, finish-sand the tray. Be careful when sanding the box-jointed corners not to burn the exposed end grain. Hand-sand the handle opening until it is smooth to the touch. Then sand a very slight round-over on all edges to break the sharp edges. Apply stain, followed by two coats of polyurethane. For added protection and a satiny feel, apply paste wax.

**Project Tool List**

Tablesaw
- Dado blade or dado set

Bandsaw or scrollsaw
Scrollsaw
Drill press
- 2½" sanding drum
- 1" drill bit

Router
- ⅛" round-over bit
- ⅜" rabbeting bit

Finishing sander

***Note:*** *We built this project using the tools listed. You may be able to substitute other tools and equipment for listed items you don't have. You'll also need various common hand tools and clamps to complete the project.*

# KITCHEN CANISTERS

**I**n Grandma's house the kitchen canisters sat at arm's length from the stove, brimming full of the ingredients she used in her daily cooking. These oak canisters will convey the same functionality and charm in your kitchen. And as a bonus, we've thrown in an easy-to-make brass scoop.

*Note: The instructions explain how to make one canister, and the Bill of Materials gives the number of pieces required for one canister. Decide on how many canisters you want, and then cut and make as many parts as necessary. If you are making more than one, we suggest you cut all identical pieces at the same time to ensure uniformity and save time.*

### Building the canister

**1.** Cut the canister back (A) to size. Using the Canister-Back

CANISTER BACK

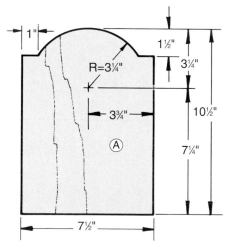

drawing *above* as a guide, lay out the radiused top edge, cut it to shape, and sand smooth.

**2.** Fit your router with a ⅜" cove bit, and rout the front top edge of the canister back where shown in the Exploded View drawing.

**3.** Cut the sides (B) to the size listed in the Bill of Materials. Then, mark and angle-cut each as follows: measure up 5⅞" from the front bottom edge of one side, and make a mark. Now, draw a line from the mark across the grain to the top back corner. Align your radial arm saw blade with the marked line, and make your cut. You can also make the cut using a tablesaw and miter gauge. Repeat for the other canister side.

**4.** Cut the canister front (C) to size plus ¼" in length. Tilt your saw blade 15° from vertical, and bevel-cut the top edge of the front to finished length (5⅞").

**5.** Cut or rout a ⅜" dado ⅜" deep ⅜" from the bottom edge of each side piece where shown on the Exploded View drawing.

**6.** Cut the bottom (D) to the size listed in the Bill of Materials. Then, cut or rout a ⅜" rabbet ⅜" deep along each edge.

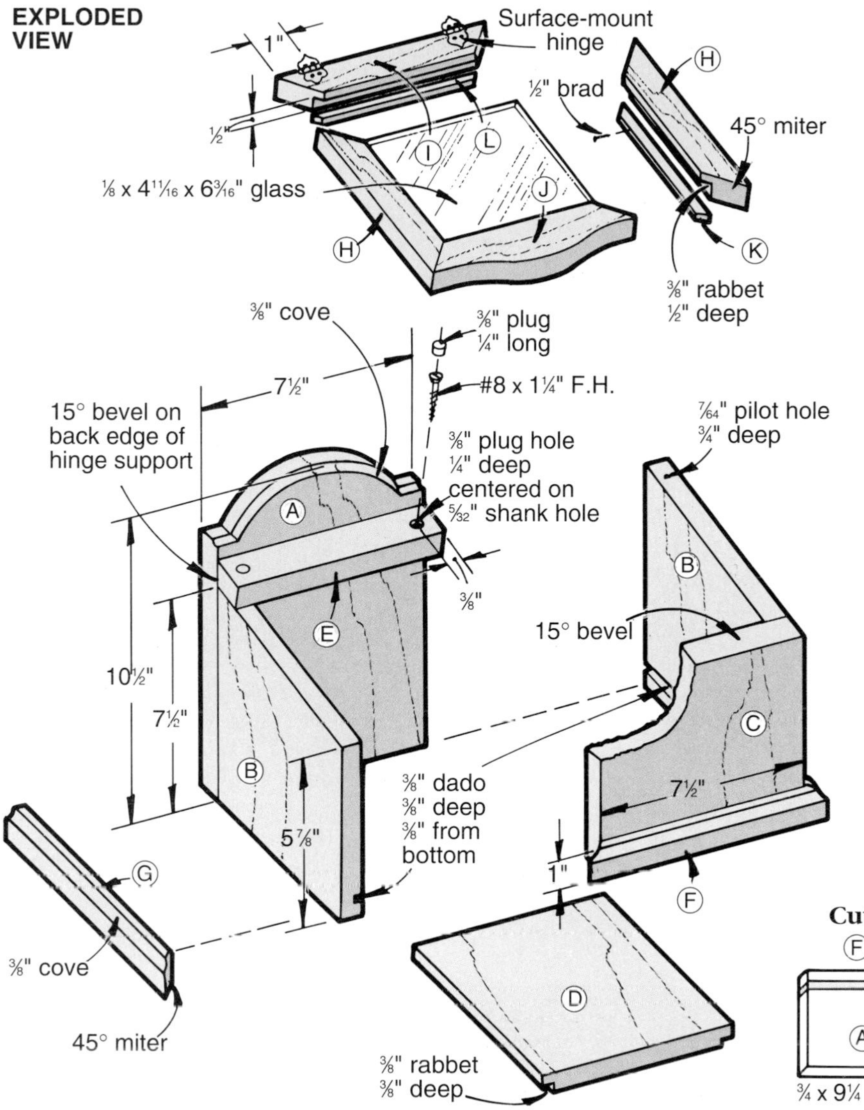
EXPLODED VIEW
1"
Surface-mount hinge
½" brad
½"
⅛ x 4 11/16 x 6 3/16" glass
45° miter
⅜" rabbet
½" deep
⅜" cove
⅜" plug
¼" long
#8 x 1¼" F.H.
7½"
15° bevel on back edge of hinge support
⅜" plug hole
¼" deep
centered on
5/32" shank hole
7/64" pilot hole
¾" deep
⅜"
15° bevel
10½"
7½"
5⅞"
⅜" dado
⅜" deep
⅜" from bottom
7½"
1"
⅜" cove
45° miter
⅜" rabbet
⅜" deep

## Bill of Materials

| Part | Finished Size* T | W | L | Mat. | Qty. |
|---|---|---|---|---|---|
| A | ¾" | 7½" | 10½" | oak | 1 |
| B | ¾" | 6" | 7½" | oak | 2 |
| C* | ¾" | 7½" | 5⅞" | oak | 1 |
| D | ¾" | 6⅝" | 6" | oak | 1 |
| E* | ¾" | 1¼" | 7½" | oak | 1 |
| F* | ½" | 1" | 8½" | oak | 1 |
| G* | ½" | 1" | 8" | oak | 2 |
| H* | 11/16" | 1" | 6" | oak | 2 |
| I* | 11/16" | 1" | 7½" | oak | 1 |
| J* | 11/16" | 1½" | 7½" | oak | 1 |
| K* | ¼" | ⅜" | 4¾" | oak | 2 |
| L* | ¼" | ⅜" | 6¼" | oak | 2 |

*Parts marked with an * are cut larger initially, and then trimmed to finished size. Please read the instructions before cutting.

**Supplies:** #8 x 1¼" flathead wood screws, ⅛ x 4 11/16 x 6 3/16" antique glass panel (available at stained glass stores), one ¾" brad for use as a drill bit, ½" brads, polyurethane, salad-bowl finish.

**Cutting Diagram** (For One Canister)

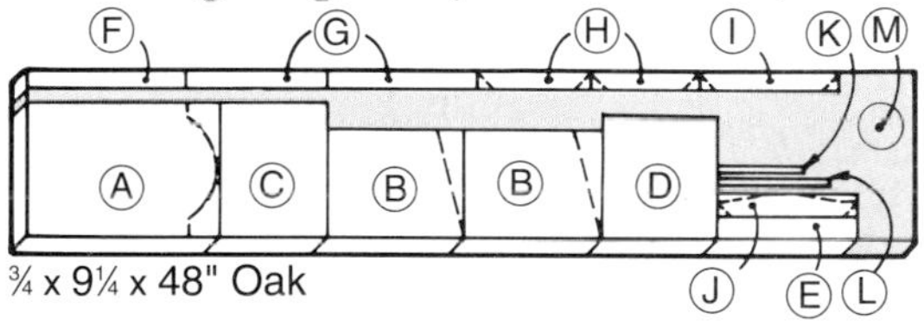
F
G
H
I
K
M
A
C
B
B
D
¾ x 9¼ x 48" Oak
J
E
L

**7.** Dry-clamp the parts together to check the fit. The bottom should fit a bit loose to allow for expansion, especially across the grain. Check the beveled top edge of the front against the angled top edge of the sides; sand or trim flush if necessary. Remove the clamps. Now, glue and clamp the canister together. Do not glue the bottom (D) in the rabbet, it "floats" freely.

**8.** Cut the hinge support (E) to size plus ¼" in width. Then, bevel-rip one edge at 15° to a finished width of 1¼". (For safety, we cut one long length for all the hinge supports; then bevel-ripped one edge of the length, and finally cut the pieces to finished length.)

**9.** Position and dry-clamp the hinge support to the canister. Now, drill the plug, shank, and pilot holes through the hinge support and into the sides (B) as dimensioned on the Exploded View drawing. Glue and screw the hinge support in place.

**10.** Plane a piece of scrap oak to 5/16" thick. Cut ⅜" oak plugs from the piece, and glue and insert them in the plug holes. Later, sand the plugs flush and the canister smooth.

### Forming and fitting the trim

**1.** Cut and shape the base molding (F, G). (We cut an oak piece ¾x1x27" for each canister, and then planed it down to ½" thick.) Rout a ⅜" cove along one edge of the long piece. Miter-cut the front (F) and sides (G) to length.

**2.** Glue and clamp the molding pieces to the base of the canister. Remove any excess glue after a tough skin has formed. Later, sand the molding smooth. (To sand the coves, we wrapped sandpaper around a ⅜" dowel.)

### Adding the lid

***Note:*** *To form a tighter seal between the canister top and lid, we applied felt tape to the lid. Applying felt to the bottom edge of the lid raises it 1/16" above the hinge support (E). To compensate, plane the lid pieces (H, I, J) to 11/16".*

*continued*

# KITCHEN CANISTERS
*continued*

**1.** To form the lid sides (H) and back (I) cut a piece of ¾" oak to 1x22" long. Cut another piece to 1½x7½" for the contoured front (J). Now, plane, joint, or resaw both pieces to ¹¹⁄₁₆".

**2.** Using carbon paper, transfer the full-sized Lid-Front Pattern *below* to a piece of paper. Use spray adhesive to stick the pattern to the lid front, and cut the contoured edge to shape (do not cut the ends yet). Sand the front edge smooth.

**3.** Cut or rout a ⅜" rabbet ½" deep along the inside edges of the lid pieces.

**4.** Miter-cut the parts (H, I, J) to the finished length listed in the Bill of Materials. Remove the paper pattern from the lid front. (We used this front as a template to mark the other fronts.)

**5.** Spread glue on the mating surfaces of the lid pieces, and bandclamp them together, checking for square.

**6.** Resaw the stops (K, L) to ¼" thick. Now, rip these to ⅜" wide and miter-cut the parts to finished length. (For safety and ease in handling, we cut long strips to thickness and width on the band saw, and then miter-cut the long pieces to length.)

## Finishing and final assembly

**1.** Finish-sand the canister and lid, sanding a very slight round-over on all sharp edges.

**2.** Have glass cut to size for each canister lid. We used hand-blown full antique glass, available at stained glass stores.

**3.** Snip the head off a ¾" brad, chuck it in your hand drill, and use it as a bit to drill pilot holes in the stops (K, L).

**4.** Position the glass in the rabbet. Nail the stops in position with ½" brads and a light hammer (9 or 10 ounces) as shown in the photo *below*. Set the brads. (Note in the photo, that we taped a piece of thin cardboard to the glass. This protects the glass when nailing and setting the brads.)

**5.** Apply the finish of your choice. (We stained our canisters first, and then applied polyurethane on the exterior and a salad-bowl finish on the inside.)

**6.** Apply self-adhesive felt tape to the underside of the lid sides and front. Also, adhere a strip of the felt tape along the back edge of the lid where shown in the drawing *below right*. See the Buying Guide for our source of felt tape.

**7.** Finally, slide the lid assembly firmly against the hinge support (E), drill pilot holes, and screw the hinges in position.

## Buying guide

• **Hinges and felt tape.** Brass-plated surface hinges (one pair per canister needed), catalog no. 27631. ¼"-wide felt tape (28" needed per canister), catalog no. 26369. For the current prices, contact The Woodworker's Store, 21801 Industrial Blvd., Rogers, MN 55374-9514, or call 612-428-3200 to order.

## Project Tool List

Tablesaw
Router
   ⅜" cove bit, ⅜" rabbeting bit
Bandsaw or scrollsaw
Drill
   Bits: ⁷⁄₆₄", ⁵⁄₃₂", ⅜"
   ⅜" plug cutter
Planer
Finishing sander

*Note: We built this project using the tools listed. You may be able to substitute other tools and equipment for listed items you don't have. You'll also need various common hand tools and clamps to complete the project.*

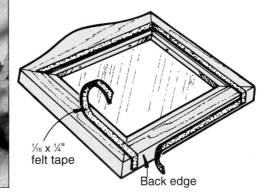

**BOTTOM SIDE OF COVER**

¹⁄₁₆ x ¼"
felt tape

Back edge

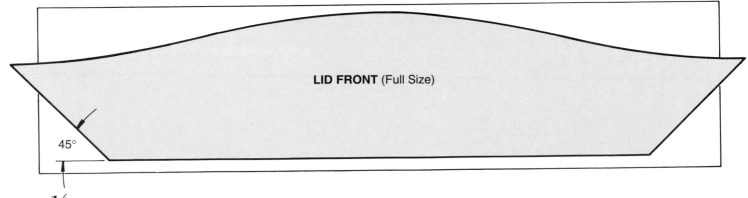

**LID FRONT** (Full Size)

45°

# BRASS SCOOP

**T**op off your canister set with our oak and brass scoop. Not only does it complement the canisters, it's super-handy for removing those vital cooking ingredients.

### Making the scoop

**1.** Plane or resaw a scrap of oak to ½" thick. Mark a 2½"-diameter circle on the ½" scrap. Cut the disk to shape for the scoop back (M). Drill a ½" hole through the center point and sand the disk smooth.

**2.** Cut a piece of ½" dowel stock to 4" long for the scoop handle (N). Sand a round-over on one end. (We sanded the round-over to shape on a belt sander.)

**3.** Glue the dowel handle in the hole in the scoop back. Later, scrape off any excess glue, finish-sand, and apply the finish.

**4.** Using carbon paper, transfer the full-sized scoop pattern and hole locations to paper, and cut the paper to shape with a scissors. Apply spray adhesive to the paper pattern, and stick it to a piece of 4x5" .010"-thick brass (most hobby stores sell thin brass sheets).

**5.** Cut the brass to shape with a scissors, and sand or file the cut edge smooth.

**6.** With the pattern still on the brass, drill the four %4" holes. Remove the paper pattern.

**7.** Roll the brass around a 16-ounce pop bottle to preform it. Now, position the rounded brass on the scoop back, and drill a ³⁄₃₂" pilot hole ½" deep into the scoop back. Fasten the brass to the scoop back with a #6x½" brass wood screw. Keeping the brass tight against the scoop back, start at one side and work your way around the disk drilling holes and fastening the brass.

### Project Tool List

Bandsaw or scrollsaw
Drill
  Bits: ³⁄₃₂", %4", ½"
Belt sander
Scissors
File

**Note:** *We built this project using the tools listed. You may be able to substitute other tools and equipment for listed items you don't have. You'll also need various common hand tools and clamps to complete the project.*

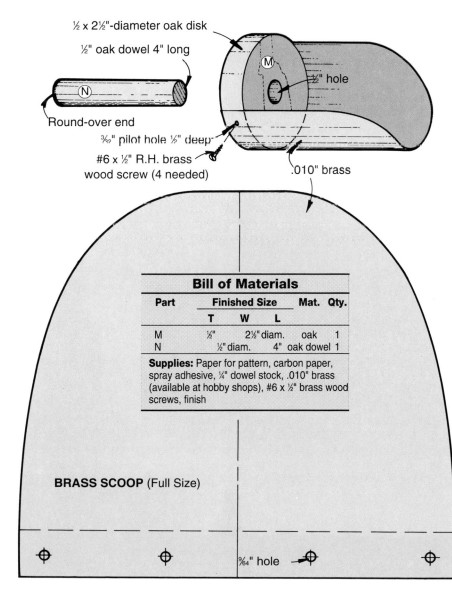

½ x 2½"-diameter oak disk

½" oak dowel 4" long

Round-over end

³⁄₃₂" pilot hole ½" deep

#6 x ½" R.H. brass wood screw (4 needed)

½" hole

.010" brass

**BRASS SCOOP** (Full Size)

%4" hole

| Bill of Materials | | | | |
|---|---|---|---|---|
| Part | Finished Size | | Mat. | Qty. |
| | T | W | L | | |
| M | ½" | 2½" diam. | | oak | 1 |
| N | ½" diam. | | 4" | oak dowel | 1 |

**Supplies:** Paper for pattern, carbon paper, spray adhesive, ¼" dowel stock, .010" brass (available at hobby shops), #6 x ½" brass wood screws, finish

# SPICE CABINET

**M**ost spice racks do an adequate job of keeping herbs and other flavorings at the ready. But this project doesn't stop here. It offers a bank of drawers and several shelves for storing your spices and displaying your favorite kitchenware. The antique glass doors and porcelain drawer knobs also add a fitting design accent to the quaint lines of the spice cabinet.

### First, construct the case

**1.** Cut the case sides (A), inner shelves (B), and lower shelf (C) to the sizes listed in the Bill of Materials plus 1/16" in width.

**2.** Using the dimensions on the Exploded View drawing, locate the four dadoes on the side pieces and cut 3/8" dadoes 3/8" deep. Now, cut a 3/8" rabbet 3/8" deep along the ends of each shelf. (We test-cut a rabbet in a piece of scrap and checked its fit in the dadoed sides first.)

**3.** Cut or rout a 1/4" rabbet 3/8" deep along the back inside edge of each side piece. (We cut our rabbets with a tablesaw. If you go this route, mount an auxiliary-wood fence to your rip fence and a dado blade set to cut 3/8" wide to the saw arbor.) Measure and position the outside edge of the dado blade 1/4" from the outside edge of the wooden fence. Start the saw and raise the blade 3/8" above the surface of the saw table and into the wood fence. Cut the rabbet as shown in photo A.

**4.** Joint, plane, or saw 1/16" off the *front* edge of sides and shelves to remove any chipping that may have occurred when you cut the dadoes and rabbets.

**5.** Using double-faced tape, stick the sides together face to face, making sure to align the dadoes and rabbet. Set your compass at 3" and lay out the radius on the lower front corner of the sides where shown in the Exploded View drawing. Cut the radius to shape, sand smooth, separate the pieces, and remove the tape.

**6.** Lay out and cut 3/4"-wide stopped dadoes 1/4" deep into the *bottom* side of the top shelf and the *top* side of the center shelf where

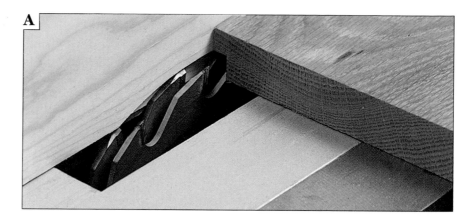

A

B

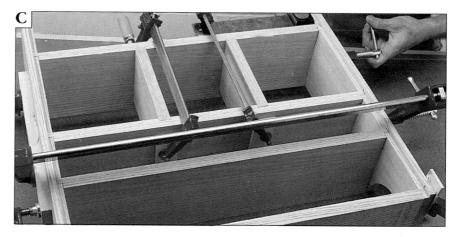

C

shown in the Exploded View drawing. Cut or rout the stopped dadoes to size. (After marking the location of the dadoes, we clamped the two shelves together with the front edge of one butting the front edge of the other. Then, we clamped a straight board to act as a fence and used a 3/4" straight bit to rout the stopped dadoes as shown in photo B.) Finally, chisel the rounded ends of the dadoes square.

**7.** Cut the dividers (D) to size. Then, dry-clamp the case together to check the fit of all joints. Remove the clamps and sand all the pieces smooth. Next, glue and clamp the parts together checking for square as shown in photo C. Also, remember to keep the shelves flush with the inside edge of the rabbet on the back edge of the sides. Remove any excess glue.

*continued*

# SPICE CABINET
*continued*

**EXPLODED VIEW**

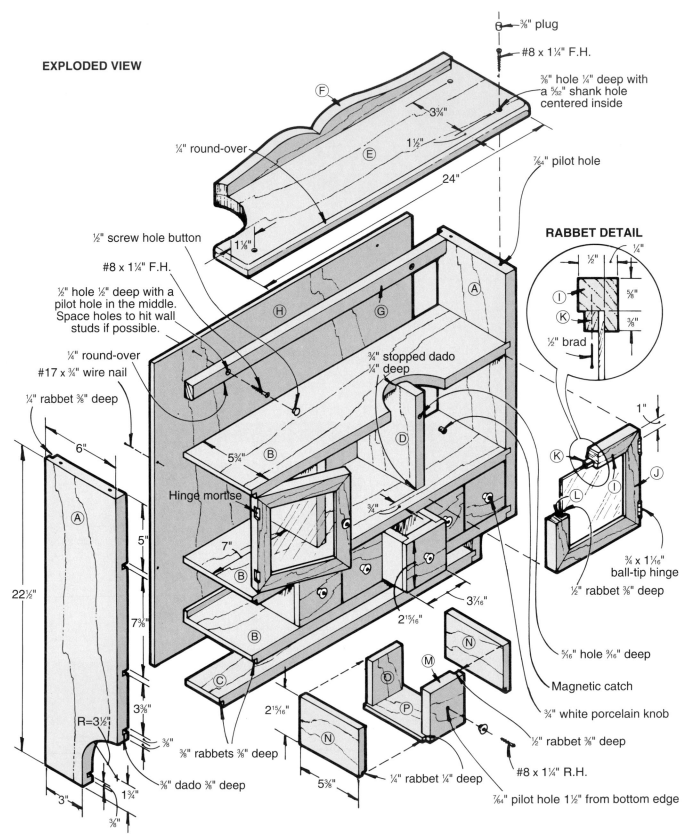

⅜" plug

#8 x 1¼" F.H.

⅜" hole ¼" deep with a ⁵⁄₃₂" shank hole centered inside

F

3¾"

1½"

¼" round-over

E

7⁄64" pilot hole

24"

½" screw hole button

1⅛"

**RABBET DETAIL**

#8 x 1¼" F.H.

A

½"  ¼"

½" hole ½" deep with a pilot hole in the middle. Space holes to hit wall studs if possible.

H  G

I

⁵⁄₈"

¼" round-over

K

⅜"

#17 x ¾" wire nail

½" brad

¼" rabbet ⅜" deep

¾" stopped dado ¼" deep

6"

1"

5¾"

B

D

K

J

Hinge mortise

¾"

I

A

5"

7"

L

B

22½"

7⅜"

B

3⁷⁄₁₆"

¾ x 1¹⁄₁₆" ball-tip hinge

2¹⁵⁄₁₆"

½" rabbet ⅜" deep

C

⁵⁄₁₆" hole ⁹⁄₁₆" deep

3⅜"

2¹⁵⁄₁₆"

N

M

Magnetic catch

R=3½"

O

¾" white porcelain knob

⅜"

P

½" rabbet ⅜" deep

3"

⅜" rabbets ⅜" deep

N

#8 x 1¼" R.H.

1¾"

5⅜"

¼" rabbet ¼" deep

⅜"

⅜" dado ⅜" deep

7⁄64" pilot hole 1½" from bottom edge

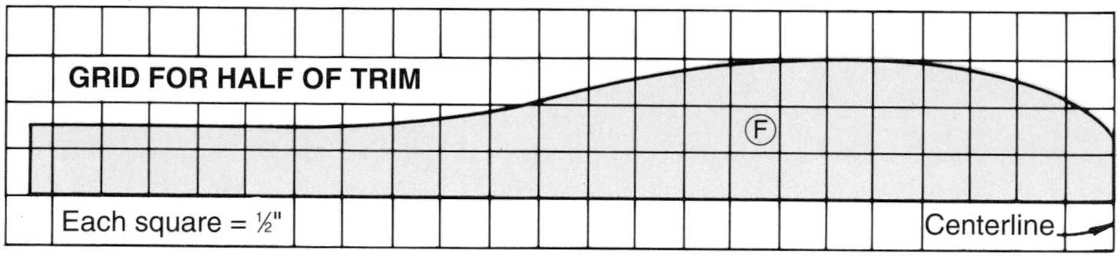

GRID FOR HALF OF TRIM
F
Each square = ½"
Centerline


**Now, add the top, trim, cleat, and back**

**1.** Cut the top of the case (E) to size. Then, rip and crosscut a piece of ¾" oak to 1½x22½" for the top trim (F). On a piece of paper draw a ½" grid. Using the Trim Grid at left as a guide, mark the points where the trim outline crosses each grid line. Connect the points to complete the pattern. Apply spray adhesive to the back of the pattern and stick it on the trim piece. Cut the trim piece to shape and remove the pattern.

**2.** Cut the cleat (G) to size. Then rout a ¼" round-over along the top (E) and cleat where shown in the Exploded View drawing.

Drill two mounting holes in the cleat. (The size and spacing of these depends on how you hang the spice shelf. Use flathead wood screws if you can locate wall studs; toggle bolts if you can't.)

**3.** Finish-sand the top of the case, the trim piece, and the cleat. Dry-clamp the top to the case with the back edges flush and a ¾" overhang at both ends. Measure in 1⅛" from the ends of the top (where shown on the Exploded View drawing), and drill plug, shank, and pilot holes to the sizes listed on the drawing. Glue and screw the top to the case. Add oak plugs and sand the surface smooth.

**4.** Glue and clamp the cleat (G) to the bottom side of the top (E) where shown on the Exploded View drawing.

**5.** Glue and clamp the trim piece (F) to the top, flush with the back edge of the top and centered from side to side.

**6.** Cut the back (H) to size from ¼" oak plywood. Check its fit in the rabbeted opening in the back of the case and set it aside for now.

*continued*

**Cutting Diagram**

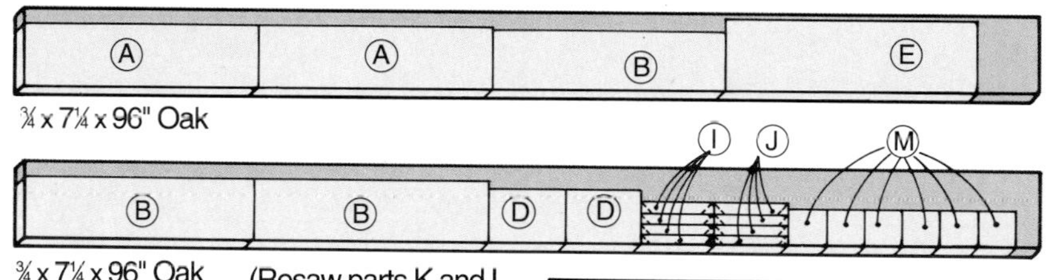

A
A
B
E
¾ x 7¼ x 96" Oak
I
J
M
B
B
D
D
¾ x 7¼ x 96" Oak
(Resaw parts K and L from the scrap of this piece.)


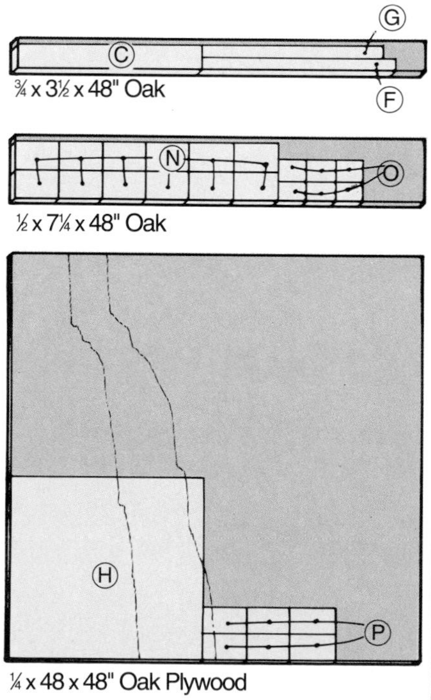

G
C
¾ x 3½ x 48" Oak
F
N
O
½ x 7¼ x 48" Oak
H
P
¼ x 48 x 48" Oak Plywood


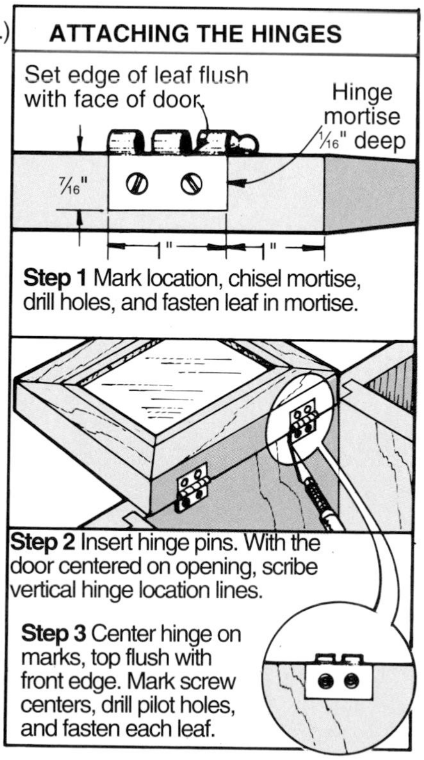

ATTACHING THE HINGES
Set edge of leaf flush with face of door
Hinge mortise 1/16" deep
7/16"
1"
1"
Step 1 Mark location, chisel mortise, drill holes, and fasten leaf in mortise.
Step 2 Insert hinge pins. With the door centered on opening, scribe vertical hinge location lines.
Step 3 Center hinge on marks, top flush with front edge. Mark screw centers, drill pilot holes, and fasten each leaf.


**Bill of Materials**

| Part | Finished Size* T | W | L | Mat. | Qty. |
|---|---|---|---|---|---|
| **THE CASE** | | | | | |
| A* | ¾" | 6" | 22½" | oak | 2 |
| B* | ¾" | 5¾" | 21¾" | oak | 3 |
| C* | ¾" | 2¾" | 21¾" | oak | 1 |
| D | ¾" | 5" | 7½" | oak | 2 |
| E | ¾" | 6¾" | 24" | oak | 1 |
| F | ¾" | 1½" | 22½" | oak | 1 |
| G | ¾" | 1" | 21" | oak | 1 |
| H | ¼" | 21¾" | 22½" | oak ply. | 1 |
| **THE TWO DOORS** | | | | | |
| I* | ¾" | 1" | 7⅜" | oak | 4 |
| J* | ¾" | 1" | 6⅞" | oak | 4 |
| K* | ¼" | ⅜" | 6⅛" | oak | 4 |
| L* | ¼" | ⅜" | 5⅝" | oak | 4 |
| **THE SIX DRAWERS** | | | | | |
| M* | ¾" | 2 15/16" | 3 7/16" | oak | 6 |
| N* | ½" | 2 15/16" | 5⅜" | oak | 12 |
| O | ½" | 2 7/16" | 2 11/16" | oak | 6 |
| P | ¼" | 2 15/16" | 5¼" | oak ply. | 6 |

*Parts marked with an * are cut larger initially, and then trimmed to finished size. Please read the instructions before cutting.

**Supplies:** double-faced tape, #8 x ¼" F.H. wood screws, #17 x ¾" wire nails, ½" brads, ½" screw hole buttons, spray adhesive, stain, polyurethane, salad bowl finish

# SPICE CABINET
*continued*

### Next, build the doors

**1.** For the door frames, cut four strips of ¾" oak 1x16" long. Now, rout or cut a ½" rabbet ⅜" deep along one edge of each piece where shown on the Rabbet Detail accompanying the Exploded View drawing. Then, miter-cut the door tops and bottoms (I) and sides (J) to finished length.

**2.** Glue and clamp each door frame together with band clamps, checking for square. Later, scrape off the excess glue.

**3.** To make the stops (K, L) from ¾" oak stock, resaw long strips to ¼" thickness, cut to ⅜" wide, and then miter-cut the stops to length.

**4.** Snip the head off a 1" brad. Chuck the brad in your drill, and use it as a bit to drill two pilot holes through each stop (K, L).

**5.** Using the three-step drawing at left as a guide, attach the hinges to the doors and then to the cabinet sides. Hang the doors.

**6.** Drill a 5⁄16" hole 5⁄16" deep in each divider (D) to accept the magnetic catches. Insert one in each hole. Close the doors almost completely, and mark where the magnetic catch makes contact with the back of each door. Remove the doors, and then drill a pilot hole and drive a mating screw for each magnetic catch.

**7.** To mount the porcelain knobs, measure up 3⅜" from the bottom of each door and drill a 7⁄64" pilot hole ½" deep for each knob. (Instead of using the machine screw that comes with the knobs, we substituted a #8x1¼" roundhead wood screw in its place.)

### Cut and assemble the drawers

**1.** Cut one piece of ¾" oak to 2¹⁵⁄16"x22" for the drawer fronts (M), and two pieces of ½" oak to 2¹⁵⁄16"x35" for the sides (N). (We planed ¾" stock down to ½" thickness for the sides and backs.)

**2.** Now, rout or cut a ¼" rabbet ¼" deep along the bottom inside edge of each of the three pieces.

**3.** Set a stop on your saw and cut the fronts 3⁷⁄16" long. Reposition the stop and cut the sides to length. Cut a ½" rabbet ⅜" deep along both ends of each drawer front.

**4.** Cut the backs (O) and bottoms (P) to finished size.

**5.** Glue and clamp the drawers together checking for square. Later, remove the clamps and check the fit of all drawers in the opening. Sand if necessary.

**6.** To locate the drawer pulls, position all the drawers in the opening, and then draw a line across the fronts 1½" up from the bottom edge of the drawer fronts. Remove the drawers, and drill a 7⁄64" pilot hole for the pulls through each front through the line and centered from side to side.

### Add the finishing touches

**1.** Remove all the hardware (except the magnetic catches—just cover them with masking tape). Then, apply stain to all the pieces, being sure to wipe on with the grain. Later, apply several coats of finish. (We applied two coats of polyurethane to the case, doors, and drawer exteriors; two coats of salad bowl finish to the drawers' interiors.)

**2.** Glue and nail the back (H) in position. Reattach the hinges and knobs. Use the technique and photo reference in the canister project to install the glass. Hang both doors.

### Buying guide

• **Hardware.** ¾"-diameter porcelain knobs, ⅜" projection (eight needed), catalog no. 35808. Round magnetic catches (two needed), catalog no. 29272. Solid brass ball-tip pin hinge, antique finish, loose pin, catalog no. 25650 (two pair needed). For current prices, contact The Woodworker's Store, 21801 Industrial Blvd., Rogers, MN 55374-9154, or call 612-428-3200 to order.

### Project Tool List
Tablesaw
    Dado blade or dado set
Bandsaw or scrollsaw
Router
    ¾" straight bit
    ¼" round-over bit
    ⅜" rabbeting bit
Drill
    Bits: 7⁄64", 5⁄16", ⅜", ½"
Jointer
Planer
Finishing sander

*Note:* We built this project using the tools listed. You may be able to substitute other tools and equipment for listed items you don't have. You'll also need various common hand tools and clamps to complete the project.

# PAPER TOWEL HOLDER

Finally, a paper-towel holder you don't have to hide under the kitchen sink! In fact, you'll want to mount it in a prominent spot to show off the intriguing wedge-key joint that secures the towel roller in place.

### Start with the end pieces

**1.** Rip and crosscut two pieces of ¾" oak to 7¼" wide by 8½" long. Then, using double-faced tape, stick the two oak pieces together face to face with the edges flush. Using the drawing of the end piece (A) on the next page as a guide, lay out the shape and hole location on one of the end pieces.

**2.** Cut the two notches in the taped-together end pieces using a table saw and miter gauge.

**3.** Drill a 1" hole through the pieces, backing the bottom piece with scrap to prevent chip-out. Using the End drawing as a guide, lay out the recess for the wedge key on one end piece and the pin on the other. Stick the end pieces to your workbench top with double-faced tape.

**4.** To form the wedge-key and dowel-pin slots, start by fitting your router with a ⅜" core-box bit set to cut to a depth of ³⁄₁₆". Attach an edge guide to your router base, and position the inside edge of the guide exactly 3¼" from the center

of the bit. As shown in the photo on page 22, rout a 2¾"-long slot for the wedge key on one of the end pieces. Flip the end pieces over, retape to the workbench, and rout a 1½"-long recess centered over the 1" hole for the ¼" dowel pin.

**5.** Cut the end pieces to shape with a bandsaw or jigsaw; then sand the contoured edges smooth. Separate the two pieces and remove the double-faced tape.

**6.** Cut a 1"-diameter dowel to 14½" long. For a smooth fit of the dowel through the 1" hole in each end piece, sand the inside of each hole larger. (We made the drum sander shown in the photo on page 23.) You can make one by cutting a 4"-long kerf in one end of a 7" length of ⅜" dowel. Cut a piece of sandpaper to 4x4", insert one end of the sandpaper into the 4" kerf, and wrap the sandpaper counterclockwise around the dowel. Secure the drum sander in the drill chuck and sand the inside of each 1" hole.

### Cutting the other parts and assembling the holder

**1.** Cut the front apron rail (B), rear rail (C), and shelf (D) to size (refer to the Front-Apron Drawing to lay out B). Clamp both rails to the end pieces. Then, drill ⅜" plug holes ½" deep through the front and rear rails where shown in the Exploded View drawing. Now, drill a ⁵⁄₃₂" shank hole through the center of the ⅜" plug holes until the drill bit makes contact with the end piece. Switch to a ⁷⁄₆₄" bit, and drill ¾" deep into each end piece, centered in each of the ⁵⁄₃₂" holes.

**2.** Remove the clamps. Measure in 2" from each end of the back rail, and drill and countersink two mounting holes. Glue and screw the rails and end pieces together. Remove any glue after it forms a tough skin.

*continued*

# PAPER TOWEL HOLDER
*continued*

**EXPLODED VIEW**

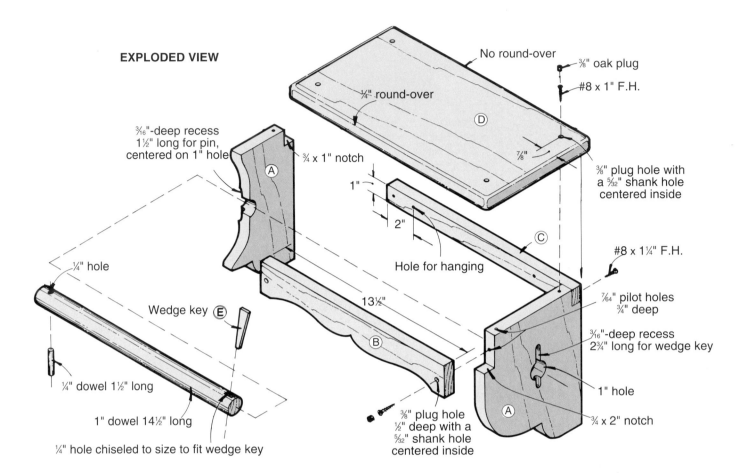

No round-over

¼" round-over

³⁄₈" oak plug

#8 x 1" F.H.

³⁄₁₆"-deep recess
1½" long for pin,
centered on 1" hole

¾ x 1" notch

(D)

1"

2"

⁷⁄₈"

³⁄₈" plug hole with
a ⁵⁄₃₂" shank hole
centered inside

(A)

(C)

¼" hole

Hole for hanging

#8 x 1¼" F.H.

Wedge key (E)

13½"

⁷⁄₆₄" pilot holes
¾" deep

¼" dowel 1½" long

(B)

³⁄₁₆"-deep recess
2¾" long for wedge key

1" dowel 14½" long

1" hole

(A)

¾ x 2" notch

¼" hole chiseled to size to fit wedge key

³⁄₈" plug hole
½" deep with a
⁵⁄₃₂" shank hole
centered inside

## Cutting Diagram

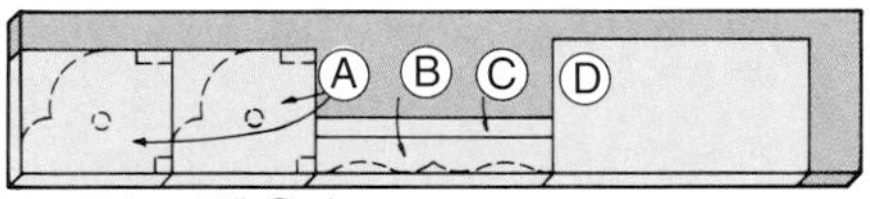

(A) (B) (C) (D)

¾ x 9¼ x 48" Oak

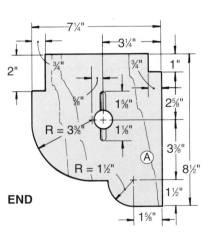

7¼"

3¼"

2"

¾"

¾"

1"

⁵⁄₈"

1⁵⁄₈"

2⁵⁄₈"

R = 3³⁄₈"

1¼"

(A)

3³⁄₈"

R = 1½"

8½"

1½"

**END**

1⁵⁄₈"

### Bill of Materials

| Part | Finished Size | | | Mat. | Qty. |
|------|------|------|------|------|------|
| | T | W | L | | |
| A | ¾" | 7¼" | 8½" | oak | 2 |
| B | ¾" | 2" | 13½" | oak | 1 |
| C | ¾" | 1" | 13½" | oak | 1 |
| D | ¾" | 7¾" | 14½" | oak | 1 |
| E | ¼" | ½" | 2" | oak | 1 |

**Supplies:** 1" oak dowel, ¼" oak dowel; double-faced tape, paraffin, #8 x 1" flathead wood screws, #8 x 1¼" flathead wood screws, stain, finish, toggle bolts

**3.** Rout a ¼" round-over along the front and side top edges of the shelf. Center the shelf on the base assembly with the back edges flush, and clamp in position. Drill the screw and plug holes— same size as those used to attach the rails—through the shelf and into the end pieces. Finally, screw the shelf to the base assembly.

**4.** Plug all the screw holes and sand the project smooth.

**5.** Insert the dowel through the end pieces, and center it in the assembly. Using the earlier cut slots as guides, mark the location of the pin and wedge-key hole locations on the dowel. Remove the dowel, and drill a ¼" hole through one end of the

dowel for the pin and another ¼" hole in the other end for the wedge key.

**6.** Cut the wedge key (E) to size using the full-sized drawing below as a guide. With a sharp ¼" chisel, form the tapered wedge-key slot in the 1" dowel to the shape shown in the drawing.

**7.** Cut a ¼" dowel to 1½" long. Center and glue it in the ¼" pin hole in the 1" dowel.

**Finishing up**

**1.** Remove the 1" dowel from the holder. Finish-sand the holder, wedge key, and dowel. Stain and finish as desired.

**2.** Using toggle bolts (for drywall), fasten the holder to the wall.

**Project Tool List**
Tablesaw
Bandsaw or scrollsaw
Router
  ⅜" core-box bit
  ¼" round-over bit
Drill
  Bits: ⁷⁄₆₄", ⁵⁄₃₂", ¼", ⅜", 1"
Finishing sander

***Note:*** *We built this project using the tools listed. You may be able to substitute other tools and equipment for listed items you don't have. You'll also need various common hand tools and clamps to complete the project.*

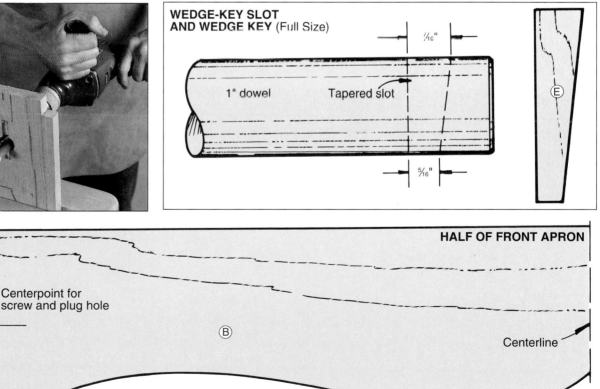

**WEDGE-KEY SLOT AND WEDGE KEY** (Full Size)

1" dowel — Tapered slot

¹⁄₁₆"

⁵⁄₁₆"

E

**HALF OF FRONT APRON**

Centerpoint for screw and plug hole

B

Centerline

# FOLDING MUFFIN STAND

A century ago in English households, women served tea and snacks to their guests from a folding muffin stand much like the one shown here. Our slightly smaller version could be the right decorative touch for entertaining, or for displaying plants in your home.

**Start by making the frame**

**1.** From ¾" pine stock, rip and crosscut two sides (A) to the dimensions listed on the Bill of Materials. See the Cutting Diagram for how we laid out and cut our material. Next, rip and crosscut the two crossbars, (B, C) to size. Rip and crosscut two 4¼x12½" blanks from the same stock for the feet (D).

**2.** Copy the patterns shown on page 27. To make a full pattern from a half-pattern, either join two pattern halves along the centerline, or fold a piece of paper and place the fold along the centerline and trace the pattern. Then, cut it to shape and unfold.

**3.** Transfer the Top Crossbar pattern and its heart-shaped opening onto the 2¾"-wide crossbar blank. Now, scrollsaw or jigsaw the piece to shape. Drill a ⅜" start hole through the heart location, and then carefully scrollsaw the heart opening to shape.

**4.** Using the dimensions on the Exploded View drawing *opposite*, locate the centerpoints for ⁵⁄₁₆" dowel holes in the ends of the top and bottom crossbars (B, C). Drill the holes ¹¹⁄₁₆" deep. (We used a centering doweling jig to help us drill these holes square.) Insert ⁵⁄₁₆" dowel centers in the dowel holes you just drilled, align the crossbars with the mating sides as shown *far right*, and press them together to mark the hole centers in the mating pieces. Drill these ⁵⁄₁₆" holes ¹¹⁄₁₆" deep also.

**5.** Mark the centerpoints for the three ⁵⁄₁₆"-diameter dowel holes on the inside edge of both sides. Drill these holes ⁷⁄₁₆" deep.

**6.** Stack the two foot blanks (D) together face-to-face with double-faced tape. Next, transfer the Foot pattern outline to the top blank. Mark the hole centerpoints. Bandsaw or scrollsaw the feet to shape. Separate the feet. Now, drill and countersink the two screw holes in each as dimensioned on the Screw Hole detail *opposite*.

**7.** Chuck a ¼" round-over bit into your router's collet. Set it to cut a bead ³⁄₃₂" deep. (We tested our setting on scrap first.) Rout along the outside edge where shown on both feet.

**8.** Rip and crosscut the leg (E) to 1¼x30". Place the Leg pattern on the side at one end of the piece, align at top and edges, and trace

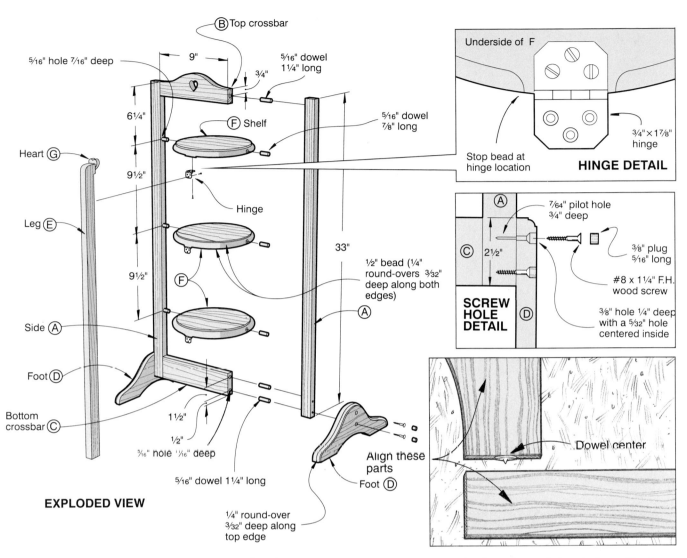

**EXPLODED VIEW**

B Top crossbar

5⁄16" hole 7⁄16" deep

9"

3⁄4"

5⁄16" dowel 1¼" long

6¼"

F Shelf

5⁄16" dowel 7⁄8" long

Heart G

9½"

Hinge

Leg E

Side A

9½"

F

33"

½" bead (¼" round-overs 3⁄32" deep along both edges)

A

Foot D

Bottom crossbar C

1½"

½"

5⁄16" hole 11⁄16" deep

5⁄16" dowel 1¼" long

¼" round-over 3⁄32" deep along top edge

Align these parts

Foot D

**HINGE DETAIL**

Underside of F

Stop bead at hinge location

¾" × 1⅞" hinge

**SCREW HOLE DETAIL**

A

C 2½"

D

7⁄64" pilot hole ¾" deep

3⁄8" plug 5⁄16" long

#8 × 1¼" F.H. wood screw

3⁄8" hole ¼" deep with a 5⁄32" hole centered inside

Dowel center

its outline. Extend the notch line to the end. Now, saw the radius and notch. (We bandsawed the radius and cut the notch on our tablesaw.)

### Next, form the round shelves

**1.** From ¾" stock, rip and crosscut three 9¼" squares. Draw diagonal lines from the corners to find the centerpoint on each. Next, scribe lines to divide each square into quarters as shown on the Shelf Blank drawing. Using the centerpoints, scribe a 9"-diameter circle (4½"-radius) on each square.

**2.** Mark the location for the 5⁄16" dowel holes on opposite edges of each square where shown on the Shelf Blank drawing. Mark the hinge position. Next, using a doweling jig, drill the two opposing dowel holes ¾" deep into the edge

of each square. For a temporary plug, crosscut six ¼" lengths of 5⁄16" dowel and insert one in each of the holes you just drilled.

**3.** Bandsaw the three shelf discs round, cutting just wide of the line. Now, sand to the line.

**4.** With the same router bit and setting as used on the feet, rout the top edge of each shelf. Next, rout along the bottom edges, stopping where the hinges will be attached as shown on the Hinge detail *above*. Remove the temporary dowel plugs from the holes in the edges of the discs. (We drilled a 1⁄16" hole into each dowel, drove a #6×1" screw part way in, and then pulled out the plugs.) Finish-sand all pieces.

### You're ready to assemble

**1.** Crosscut six 7⁄8" lengths of 5⁄16" dowel and insert them in the holes

in the edges of the shelves. Next, dry-assemble the frame and shelves (A, B, C, and F) to test the fit. Adjust parts if necessary to fit. Now, glue and assemble the frame, incorporating the shelves before adding the second side. Clamp and square the frame. Do not glue the shelf dowels; they should turn freely.

**2.** To attach the feet, first make the Squaring Jig shown on page 26. (We made ours from scrap particleboard.) Use the jig as shown on page 26 to square the feet to the frame. With the jig holding the foot and leg square, drill through the existing feet holes to form pilot holes in the frame. Glue and screw both feet to the frame with #8×1¼" flathead wood screws.

**3.** With a 3⁄8" plug cutter, cut four plugs from scrap pine. Glue one in *continued*

# FOLDING MUFFIN STAND
*continued*

**SHELF BLANK**

Draw diagonals to locate center

9¼"

9¼"

R=4½"

Ⓕ

5/16" holes ¾" deep drilled on opposite sides

3/8"

Hinge location

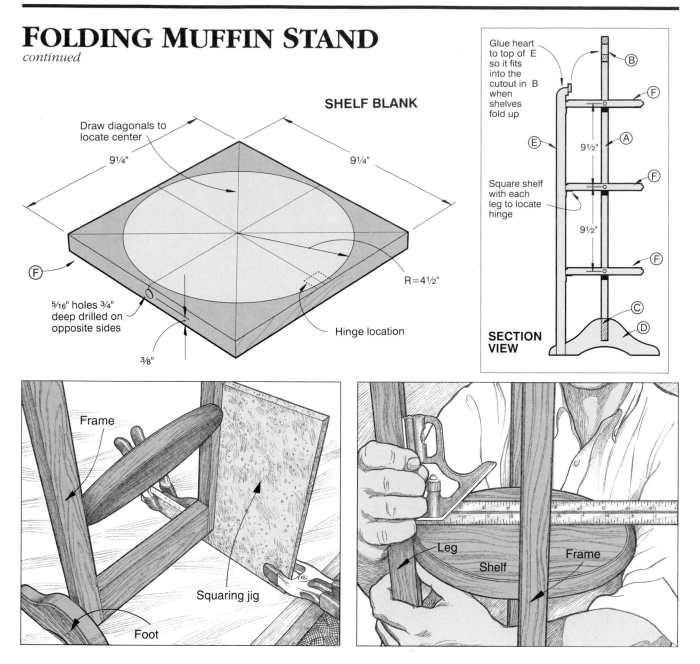

Glue heart to top of E so it fits into the cutout in B when shelves fold up

Ⓑ

Ⓕ

Ⓔ

Ⓐ

9½"

Square shelf with each leg to locate hinge

Ⓕ

9½"

Ⓕ

Ⓒ

Ⓓ

**SECTION VIEW**

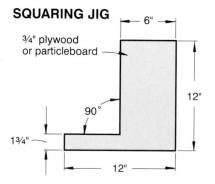

Frame

Squaring jig

Foot

Leg

Shelf

Frame

## SQUARING JIG

¾" plywood or particleboard

6"

12"

90°

1¾"

12"

each of the counterbored screw holes in the feet. Trim and sand the plugs flush with the surface.

**4.** To position the hinges on the shelves and leg, first apply a strip of double-faced tape to the hinges. Next, using the Section View drawing *top right* as a guide, and a square as shown *above*, square the shelves to the leg, position the hinges, and then mark the hinge's screw-hole centers. Drill the pilot holes, and then attach the hinges. (We had to bend the hinges in slightly at the knuckle so the shelves would fold up properly.)

**5.** Transfer the small Heart pattern to a piece of ¼"-thick pine. Scrollsaw it to shape and then glue it to the leg top so it insets in the heart opening of the crossbar when the shelves fold to the vertical position.

**6.** Apply the finish of your choice. Our project painter, Susan Henry, first sealed the wood with a clear wood sealer. Next, she mixed 3 parts Raw Sienna and 1 part Burnt Sienna thinned with odorless turpentine. (You can buy the products listed here at most crafts-supply stores.) She applied this stain mixture to the front, back, and inside surfaces of the frame, and the tops and bottoms of each shelf. The remaining edges were painted with Peach acrylic paint. When dry, Susan sealed the finished surfaces with Krylon matte 1311. For the shelf top trim, Susan designed and then cut her own stencil from Mylar. She painted the Peach colored hearts and dots first, then the Green strokes and dots. After these paints dried, she sealed them with a light coat of waterbased varnish.

## Project Tool List

Tablesaw
Bandsaw
Scrollsaw
Router
    ¼" round-over bit
Drill
    Bits: 1/16", 7/64", 5/32", 5/16", 3/8"
    3/8" plug cutter
Finishing sander

*Note: We built this project using the tools listed. You may be able to substitute other tools and equipment for listed items you don't have. You'll also need various common hand tools and clamps to complete the project.*

### Bill of Materials

| Part | Finished Size* | | | Mat. | Qty. |
|------|------|------|------|------|------|
| | T | W | L | | |
| A side | ¾" | 1¼" | 33" | P | 2 |
| B top crossbar | ¾" | 2¾" | 9" | P | 1 |
| C crossbar | ¾" | 2½" | 9" | P | 1 |
| D foot | ¾" | 4⅛" | 12½" | P | 2 |
| E leg | ¾" | 1¼" | 30" | P | 1 |
| F* shelf | ¾" | | 9" dia. | P | 3 |
| G* heart | ¼" | 1" | 1" | P | 1 |

*Parts marked with * cut to final size during construction. Please read instructions before cutting.

**Material key:** P-pine
**Supplies:** ¾ x 1⅞" brass ornamental hinges (Stanley catalog no. CD5311 US3), 5/16" dowel, #8 x 1¼" flathead wood screws, paint and finish.

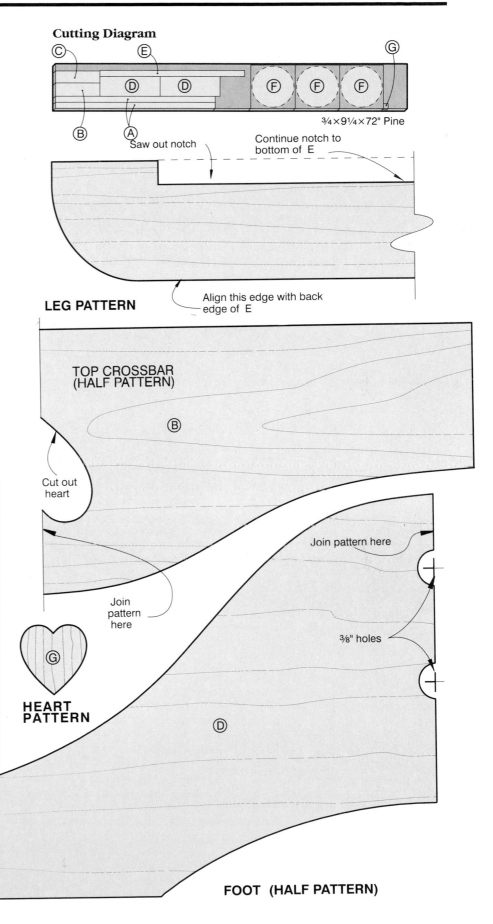

**Cutting Diagram**

¾×9¼×72" Pine

Saw out notch

Continue notch to bottom of E

**LEG PATTERN**

Align this edge with back edge of E

**TOP CROSSBAR (HALF PATTERN)**

Cut out heart

Join pattern here

Join pattern here

3/8" holes

**HEART PATTERN**

**FOOT (HALF PATTERN)**

# THE ORGANIZED COOK'S COMPANION

**F**or those who insist on a place for everything and everything in its place.

### Cut the cabinet parts first

**1.** Make a Side pattern using the gridded pattern *below right* as your guide. (To manually enlarge this gridded pattern, we first drew ½" squares across our paper, then plotted the points where the pattern lines cross grid lines. Next, we connected the points. When a part has curves like this piece, we use French curves to draw smooth-flowing lines. Or, you can increase the pattern on an enlarging-type photocopier.)

**2.** From ¾"-thick oak, crosscut a 14"-long piece. (As shown by the Cutting Diagram on page 31, we started with a 9¼"-wide board.) Square both ends. Now, adhere your Side pattern to the face of the piece, aligning its square corner with a square corner on the oak.

**3.** Bandsaw the side (A) to shape, cutting just outside the line. Next, use the piece you cut out as a pattern and scribe the outline of a second side onto the remaining portion of the 14" length. Bandsaw it to shape. Now using double-faced tape, stack the two sides together face-to-face, aligning both straight edges. Sand the curved edges to the pattern line. (For this operation we used the rounded end on our stationary belt sander.)

**4.** Drill the two ⅜" holes through the sides where indicated on the pattern. (We placed a scrap of wood under the sides when drilling to prevent chip-out.) Separate the sides and remove the tape and pattern. (We used lacquer thinner to help dissolve the adhesive.)

**5.** Rip and crosscut two shelves (B) to the dimensions listed on the Shelf drawing *opposite*. Rip and crosscut two spacers (C) to the dimensions listed on the Bill of Materials. Next, rip and crosscut one front spanner (D), and one back spanner (E) to dimension. (We overcut the length of both spanners by ¼" in order to fit them precisely during assembly.) Now, finish-sand all cabinet pieces. (We used 120-, 180-, and 220-grit sandpapers.)

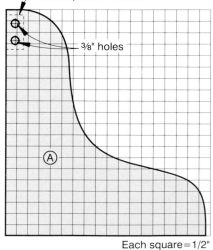

Back spanner location

⅜" holes

Ⓐ

Each square = 1/2"

**SIDE (Gridded Pattern)**

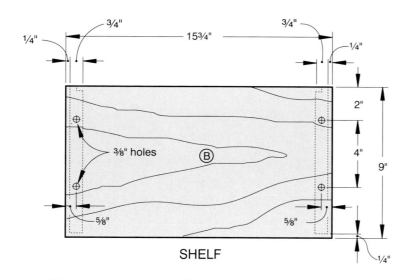

**SHELF**

Dimensions shown: 1/4", 3/4", 15¾", 3/4", 1/4", 2", 4", 9", 5/8", 5/8", 1/4", ⅜" holes, Ⓑ

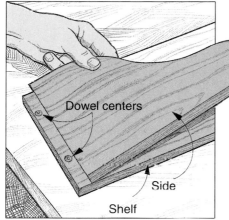

Dowel centers
Side
Shelf

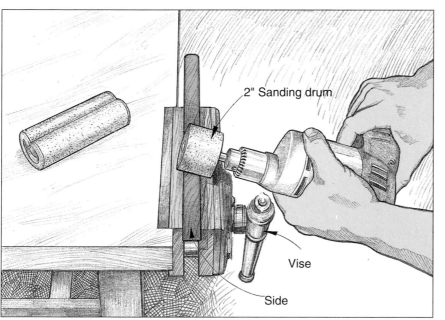

2" Sanding drum
Vise
Side

**6.** Stack and tape the two shelves face-to-face, aligning the edges. For orientation, make a faint pencil line across the back edges of both. Locate the centerpoints for the four ⅜" holes on the face of the top. Drill through the top shelf and ½" into the bottom one. Separate the shelves.

**7.** Place ⅜" dowel centers in the top holes of the top shelf. One by one, position the sides (A) on the shelf, align as shown *left*, and

then press down on the sides to mark the centers of the mating holes in the sides. (We also drew guidelines on the parts to help align the holes.) Using a dowling jig, drill the ⅜" holes you just marked 1" deep into the bottom edge of both of the sides (A).

**8.** Place the dowel-hole centers in the holes in the underside of the top shelf and mark the hole centerpoints in the top edge of both spacers (C). Using the same technique, mark the centerpoints for the mating holes in the bottom edge of the spacers and bottom shelf. Drill the ⅜" holes ½" deep into the edges of both spacers where you've marked them.

**9.** Set up your table-mounted router as shown on the Edge Round detail *below*. Next, round over the front edge and ends on both shelves (B). Do not rout the back edges on either piece. Now, sand a matching round-over along the curved front edge of both sides (A) using the technique shown *below left*.

**EDGE ROUND DETAIL**

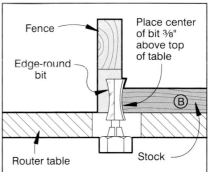

Fence
Place center of bit ⅜" above top of table
Edge-round bit
Ⓑ
Router table
Stock

**Assemble the cabinet now**

**1.** Crosscut four ⅜" dowels ⅞" long, and glue them in the holes in the bottom shelf. Cut four ⅜" dowels 1¾" long, and glue them in the holes in the top edge of the spacers. Next, glue the top and bottom shelves to the spacers. Note: The dowels extend through the top shelf. Clamp the assembly and square. (We cut a scrap piece to fit tightly in the opening and to hold the box square.) Wipe off the glue squeeze-out. Remove the clamps after the glue cures.

*continued*

# THE ORGANIZED COOK'S COMPANION

*continued*

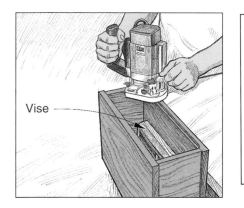

Vise

## BACK RABBET DETAIL

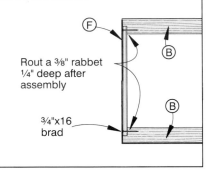

Rout a ⅜" rabbet ¼" deep after assembly

¾"x16 brad

### Bill of Materials

| Part | Finished Size* | | | Mat. | Qty. |
|---|---|---|---|---|---|
| | T | W | L | | |
| **Cabinet** | | | | | |
| A side | ¾" | 8¾" | 10" | O | 2 |
| B shelf | ¾" | 9 " | 15¾" | O | 2 |
| C spacer | ¾" | 8¾" | 4⅞" | O | 2 |
| D*fr. spanner | ¾" | ¾" | 13¾" | O | 1 |
| E*bk.spanner | ¾" | 1½" | 13¾" | O | 1 |
| F* back | ¼" | 5⅝" | 14½" | OP | 1 |
| **Drawers** | | | | | |
| G front | ¾" | 4" | 6¾" | O | 2 |
| H side | ¾" | 3½" | 8" | O | 4 |
| I back | ¾" | 4¼" | 6⅛" | O | 2 |
| J bottom | ⅛" | 6½" | 8" | H | 2 |

*Parts marked with an * will be cut to fit during construction. Please read the instructions before cutting.

**Material key:** O-oak; OP-oak plywood; H-hardboard

**Supplies:** ⅜" dowel, 4d nails, ¾" x 16 brads, #8 x 2" roundhead brass wood screws, two drawer pulls.

**2.** Chuck a ⅜"-piloted rabbeting bit into your handheld router and set it to cut ¼" deep. Clamp the box in a vise back-side up, and as shown *above*, rout a rabbet around the inside edge of the box. See the Back Rabbet detail *above right* for information. Chisel the round rabbet corners square. Now, rip and crosscut the back (F) to fit the rabbeted opening. (We used ¼" oak plywood, but hardboard would work.) Finally, glue and nail the back in place.

**3.** Glue and clamp the sides (A) to the box assembled in Step 1. Fit the back spanner between the sides and crosscut it to final length. Place it in position, and then drill through the existing holes in each side and ¾" into the ends of the spanner. Glue a ⅜x1½" dowel in each hole. Sand the dowel ends flush with each side.

**4.** Crosscut the front spanner (D) to fit between the spacers. Glue it in place where shown on the Exploded View drawing *opposite*.

## Complete the drawers and then finish the recipe box

*Note: We designed the drawers so you can't accidentally pull them all the way out of the shelf—and spill the cards.*

**1.** From ¾" stock, rip and crosscut two drawer fronts (G) to dimension. Next, rip and crosscut four drawer sides (H) and two drawer backs (I) to dimension. See the Drawer Assembly drawing *below* for additional details.

**2.** To cut the rabbets on the drawer fronts, study the Drawer Assembly drawing carefully. Set the rip fence ¾" to the left of the saw blade. Elevate the blade to ⅜" above the saw table. Now, saw a ⅛"-wide kerf on both ends of both fronts and on one end of each side piece (H).

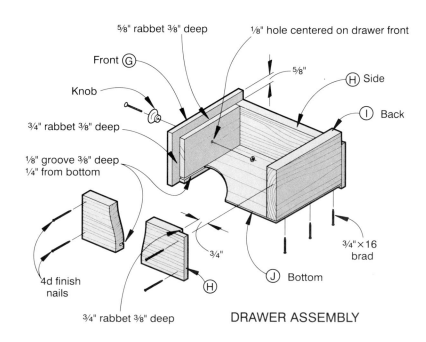

⅝" rabbet ⅜" deep

⅛" hole centered on drawer front

Front G

⅝"

H Side

Knob

I Back

¾" rabbet ⅜" deep

⅛" groove ⅜" deep ¼" from bottom

¾"

¾"×16 brad

4d finish nails

H

J Bottom

¾" rabbet ⅜" deep

**DRAWER ASSEMBLY**

**3.** Set the fence ¼" to the right of the blade and make ⅛" kerfs for your drawer bottoms in both fronts and the four drawer sides. Next, set the fence ⅝" to the left of the saw blade. Now, saw a kerf along the top inside edge of the two fronts.

**4.** Set the fence ⅜" to the right of the blade and then elevate the blade to ⅝" above the saw table. Turn the fronts on edge and saw along the top edge to complete the top rabbet. Now, elevate the blade to ¾" above the saw table. Cut along the ends of both fronts to finish forming the rabbets on the ends of the two fronts. Finally, do the same operation to one end on each of the sides.

**5.** Draw diagonal lines on the drawer fronts to locate the centerpoint. Drill a ⅛" hole through both fronts for the knob screws.

**6.** Glue and nail the drawers together. (We used 4d finish nails.) Square the drawers and clamp while the glue dries. Measure and then cut the bottom (J) for each drawer from ⅛" hardboard. Slide the bottom panels into the grooves in the sides. Next, apply a light film of glue along the bottom edge of the back and nail the bottom to it with ¾"×16 brads.

**7.** Apply the finish of your choice. (We wiped on a medium-oak oil stain. After it dried, we applied one coat of lacquer sanding sealer and two coats of clear semigloss lacquer, sanding between coats with 320-grit sandpaper to level the surfaces.) Attach drawer pulls of your choice.

**8.** If you wish to wall-mount the recipe box, drill two 5⁄32" holes through the back spanner where shown. Attach the rack to the wall with #8×2" roundhead or ovalhead brass wood screws. Use other wall fasteners in areas where screws do not penetrate wall studs.

**Project Tool List**
Tablesaw
Bandsaw
Belt sander
Drill
  Bits: ⅛", 5⁄32", ⅜"
  2" drum sander
Router
  Router table
  Edge-round bit
  ⅜" rabbeting bit
  Finishing sander

*Note: We built this project using the tools listed. You may be able to substitute other tools and equipment for listed items you don't have. You'll also need various common hand tools and clamps to complete the project.*

**Cutting Diagram**

3⁄4×9¼×96" Oak

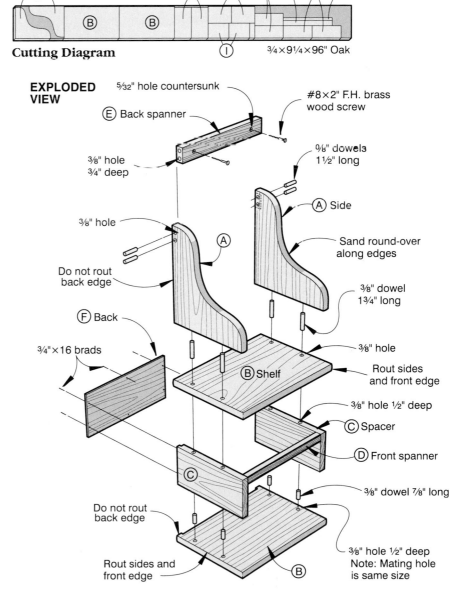

**EXPLODED VIEW**

5⁄32" hole countersunk

E Back spanner

#8×2" F.H. brass wood screw

⅜" hole 3⁄4" deep

⅜" dowels 1½" long

⅜" hole

Do not rout back edge

A Side

Sand round-over along edges

A

⅜" dowel 1¾" long

F Back

3⁄4"×16 brads

⅜" hole

Rout sides and front edge

B Shelf

⅜" hole ½" deep

C Spacer

D Front spanner

C

⅜" dowel 7⁄8" long

Do not rout back edge

Rout sides and front edge

B

⅜" hole ½" deep Note: Mating hole is same size

**31**

# COUNTRY GOOSE NAPKIN HOLDER

**T**ake a gander at this accommodating accent for your kitchen table. It combines two well-loved country symbols—a goose and a heart—into a practical accessory.

Transfer the full-sized goose pattern on the opposite page onto ½"-thick stock and the heart pattern onto ¼" stock (we used clear white pine). To keep the neck portion strong follow the grain direction on the Exploded View drawing when laying out the pieces. With bandsaw fitted with a ⅛" blade or a scrollsaw with a #9 skip-tooth blade, cut out the geese and heart shapes. (Double-faced tape allowed us to stack and cut out the geese and hearts in pairs.) From ¾" stock, cut the bottom of the holder to 2x4¾". Cut or sand the ends of the divider to the same shape as the goose outline. Then, drill a pair of ⅛" holes ½" deep in each heart where located on the full-sized pattern. Sand the parts.

For the best results, paint the geese before assembly, but mask the areas that will contact the base. (To paint the pieces, we used water-based acrylics and a no. 6 sable brush.) Apply the gray (a mixture of black and white), the black, and finally the white. Paint the hearts red.

To achieve the aged look, lightly sand the edges of each goose and heart after the paint has dried. To further age the project, rub on a brown-colored stain (we used a waterbased acrylic) and immediately wipe off most of it. Using a ¼" brad-point bit, form a slight depression for each eye.

Glue the divider between the goose pieces: Cut two pieces of thin jute cord to 6½ " long. Glue the ends of each cord into the holes in the heart. Hang the hearts around each goose neck, and fill the holder with napkins.

**Project Tool List**
Tablesaw
Bandsaw or scrollsaw
Belt sander
Drill
   Bit: ⅛"

**Note:** *We built this project using the tools listed. You may be able to substitute other tools and equipment for listed items you don't have. You'll also need various common hand tools and clamps to complete the project.*

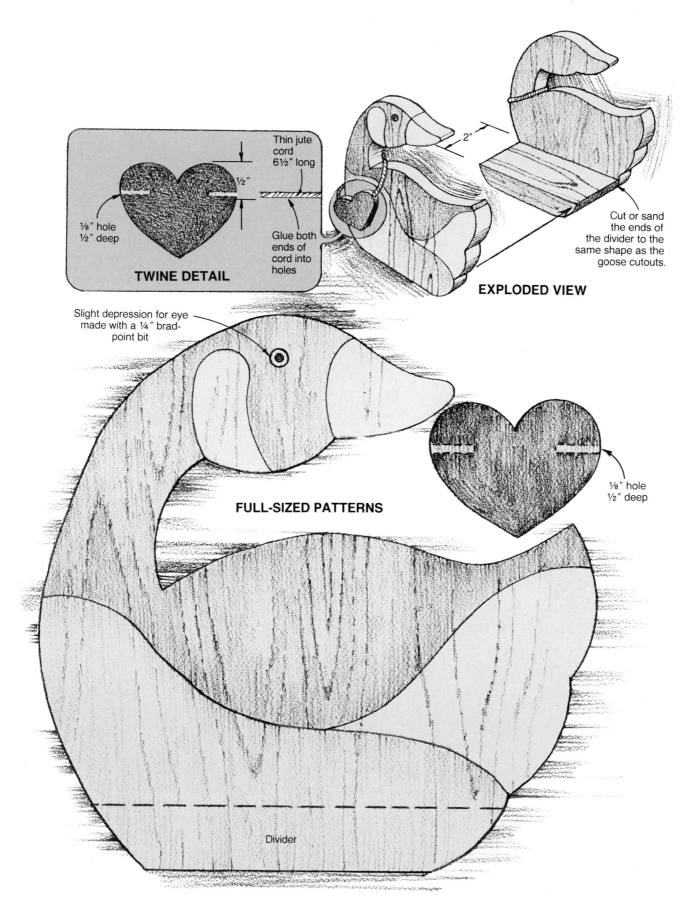

**TWINE DETAIL**

Thin jute cord 6½" long

½"

⅛" hole ½" deep

Glue both ends of cord into holes

**EXPLODED VIEW**

2"

Cut or sand the ends of the divider to the same shape as the goose cutouts.

Slight depression for eye made with a ¼" brad-point bit

**FULL-SIZED PATTERNS**

⅛" hole ½" deep

Divider

# DOWN-HOME DISPLAYS AND ACCESSORIES

*The projects that follow are meant for show. Display your favorite woodcrafts on the wall or in any of the charming cabinets we've designed for you.*

# PRIZEWINNING PLATE RACK

**H**ere's a winner. The editors of *Plate World*, a magazine for decorative-plate collectors, headquartered in Niles, Illinois, pinned the blue ribbon for the magazine's "Do-It-Yourself Display" contest on this corner plate holder. Timothy Burke of Ramsey, Minnesota, designed and built the original as a four-plate display; we've scaled it down to show off one 8½" plate. But who's to stop you from building a batch of them?

Enlarge the half-pattern, *right,* on gridded paper or by photocopying at the percentages indicated. Select two boards ¾x9x14" (glue up narrower stock, if necessary ) and one ¾x4½x12" for each single-plate holder. (We used red oak.)

Joint one edge of each wide piece, and then stack both together with double-faced tape. Make sure to align the jointed edges. Crosscut the boards to 13³⁄₁₆", and then attach the pattern to the top piece with spray adhesive.

With a Forstner bit or spade bit chucked into a drill press, bore 1¼" holes where shown on the pattern. Bandsaw around the pattern line. Now, mark the center on one end of the ¾x4½x12" board. With your tablesaw miter gauge set at 45°, saw one corner off the board, starting from the center mark. Then, flip the board over and repeat the cut. Affix the enlarged Plate Support pattern to the piece, aligning the right angle with the one on the workpiece. Bandsaw the plate support.

Drill the holes for the Shaker pegs where shown. Then, chuck a sanding drum in your drill press, and sand all edges. Install a ¼" beading bit in your table-mounted router, and then rout along the

*continued*

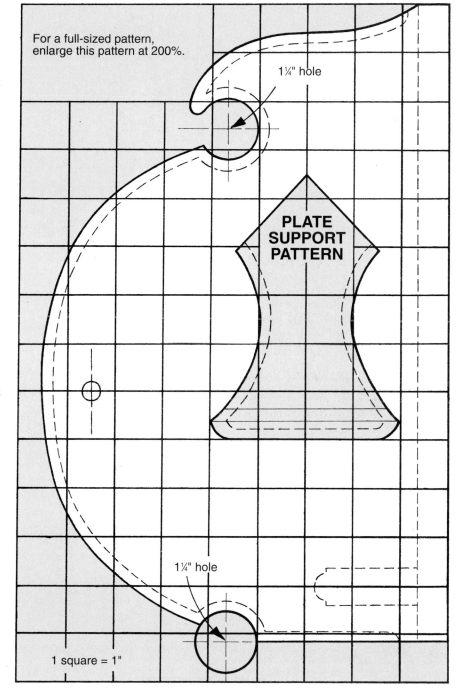

For a full-sized pattern, enlarge this pattern at 200%.

1¼" hole

**PLATE SUPPORT PATTERN**

1¼" hole

1 square = 1"

# PRIZEWINNING PLATE RACK
*continued*

front edge of each side piece where shown on the Exploded View drawing. *Stop the cut ⅞" from the back edge of each board at both top and bottom.* With a hanging-slot bit, rout a slot centered near the top on back of each piece.

Change to a ¼" beading bit. Adjust the router depth to cut a bead ¹⁄₁₆" deep. Then, rout the plate support along both edges where shown. Refer to the Routing the Dado drawing to rout the plate groove with a ¼" straight bit.

Cut ¾" off the back edge of the right side piece. When setting your saw fence for this cut, be sure to measure to the edge of the blade away from the fence. Position the blade as low as possible, and use your pushstick when making this cut.

Drill screw holes where shown on the Exploded View drawing. Sand all parts before you assemble the two sides and plate support with screws and glue. Glue the Shaker pegs into place, and then apply your favorite finish.

### Project Tool List
Tablesaw
Bandsaw
Drill
Drill press
   Bits: ⁷⁄₆₄", ⁵⁄₃₂", ⅜", 1¼"
Sanding drum
Router
   Router table
   ¼" beading bit
   ¼" straight bit
Finishing sander

**Note:** *We built this project using the tools listed. You may be able to substitute other tools and equipment for listed items you don't have. You'll also need various common hand tools and clamps to complete the project.*

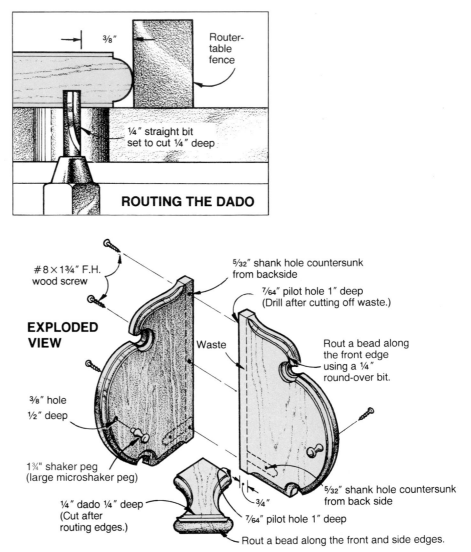

**ROUTING THE DADO**

3/8"
Router-table fence
¼" straight bit set to cut ¼" deep

**EXPLODED VIEW**

#8 × 1¾" F.H. wood screw
⁵⁄₃₂" shank hole countersunk from backside
⁷⁄₆₄" pilot hole 1" deep (Drill after cutting off waste.)
Waste
Rout a bead along the front edge using a ¼" round-over bit.
⅜" hole ½" deep
1¾" shaker peg (large microshaker peg)
¼" dado ¼" deep (Cut after routing edges.)
¾"
⁵⁄₃₂" shank hole countersunk from back side
⁷⁄₆₄" pilot hole 1" deep
Rout a bead along the front and side edges.

# CHERRY WALL CABINET

C lean and simple with a Shaker air about it, our cherry wall cabinet makes a nice addition to most any wall in need of dressing up. You can build it in two evenings and enjoy it for a lifetime.

*Note: You'll need some thin stock for this project. You can either resaw or plane thicker stock to size.*

**Start with the basic case**

**1.** From ¾"-thick cherry cut the sides (A), fixed shelf (B), and top and bottom (C) to the sizes listed in the Bill of Materials.

**2.** Mark the locations and cut a ¾" dado ¼" deep on the inside face of each cabinet side. Then, cut or rout a ⅜" rabbet ¼" deep along the back inside edge of each cabinet side.

**3.** Mark the shelf-hole centerpoints and drill ¼" holes ½" deep on the inside face of the side pieces (40 holes total).

**4.** After viewing the Chamfer detail for reference, rout a chamfer along the front and side edges of the top and bottom pieces (C).

**5.** Sand the cabinet pieces. Now, dry-clamp the cabinet with the back edges flush; check for square. Mark the dowel-hole centerpoints on the top and bottom pieces, and drill ⅜" holes through the top and bottom and 1" into the ends of the side pieces. Remove the clamps.

**6.** Cut eight ⅜"-diameter dowels 1¾" long (we used cherry dowel stock; see the Buying Guide for our source). Next, glue, dowel, and clamp the cabinet assembly (A, B, C), checking for square. Wipe off excess glue with a damp cloth. Trim and sand the protruding end of each dowel flush with the cabinet surface.

**7.** Mark the location and fasten the hinges to the cabinet side. (See the Buying Guide for our source of hardware.)

*continued*

# CHERRY WALL CABINET

*continued*

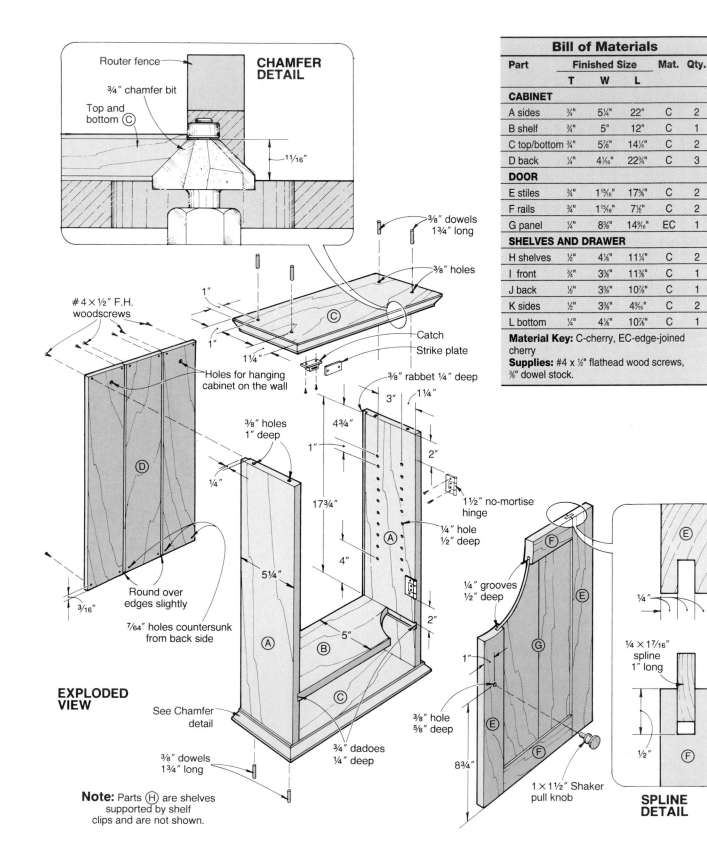

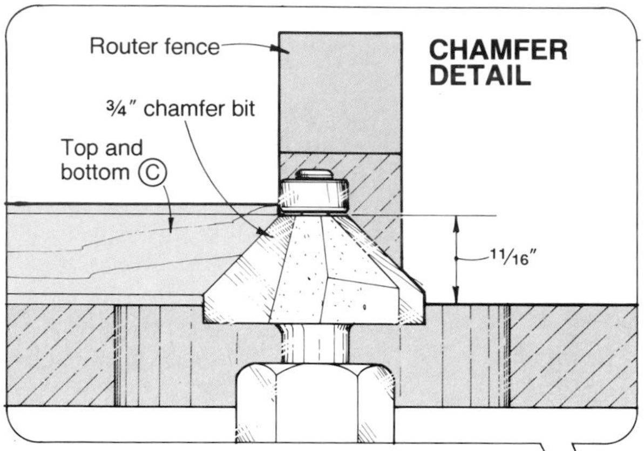
CHAMFER DETAIL
Router fence
3/4" chamfer bit
Top and bottom (C)
11/16"

| Part | Finished Size T | W | L | Mat. | Qty. |
|---|---|---|---|---|---|
| **CABINET** | | | | | |
| A sides | 3/4" | 5 1/4" | 22" | C | 2 |
| B shelf | 3/4" | 5" | 12" | C | 1 |
| C top/bottom | 3/4" | 5 7/8" | 14 1/4" | C | 2 |
| D back | 1/4" | 4 1/16" | 22 3/4" | C | 3 |
| **DOOR** | | | | | |
| E stiles | 3/4" | 1 15/16" | 17 5/8" | C | 2 |
| F rails | 3/4" | 1 15/16" | 7 1/2" | C | 2 |
| G panel | 1/4" | 8 3/8" | 14 9/16" | EC | 1 |
| **SHELVES AND DRAWER** | | | | | |
| H shelves | 1/2" | 4 1/8" | 11 1/4" | C | 2 |
| I front | 3/4" | 3 3/8" | 11 3/8" | C | 1 |
| J back | 1/2" | 3 3/8" | 10 7/8" | C | 1 |
| K sides | 1/2" | 3 3/8" | 4 9/16" | C | 2 |
| L bottom | 1/4" | 4 1/8" | 10 7/8" | C | 1 |

Table: **Bill of Materials**

**Material Key:** C-cherry, EC-edge-joined cherry
**Supplies:** #4 x 1/2" flathead wood screws, 3/8" dowel stock.

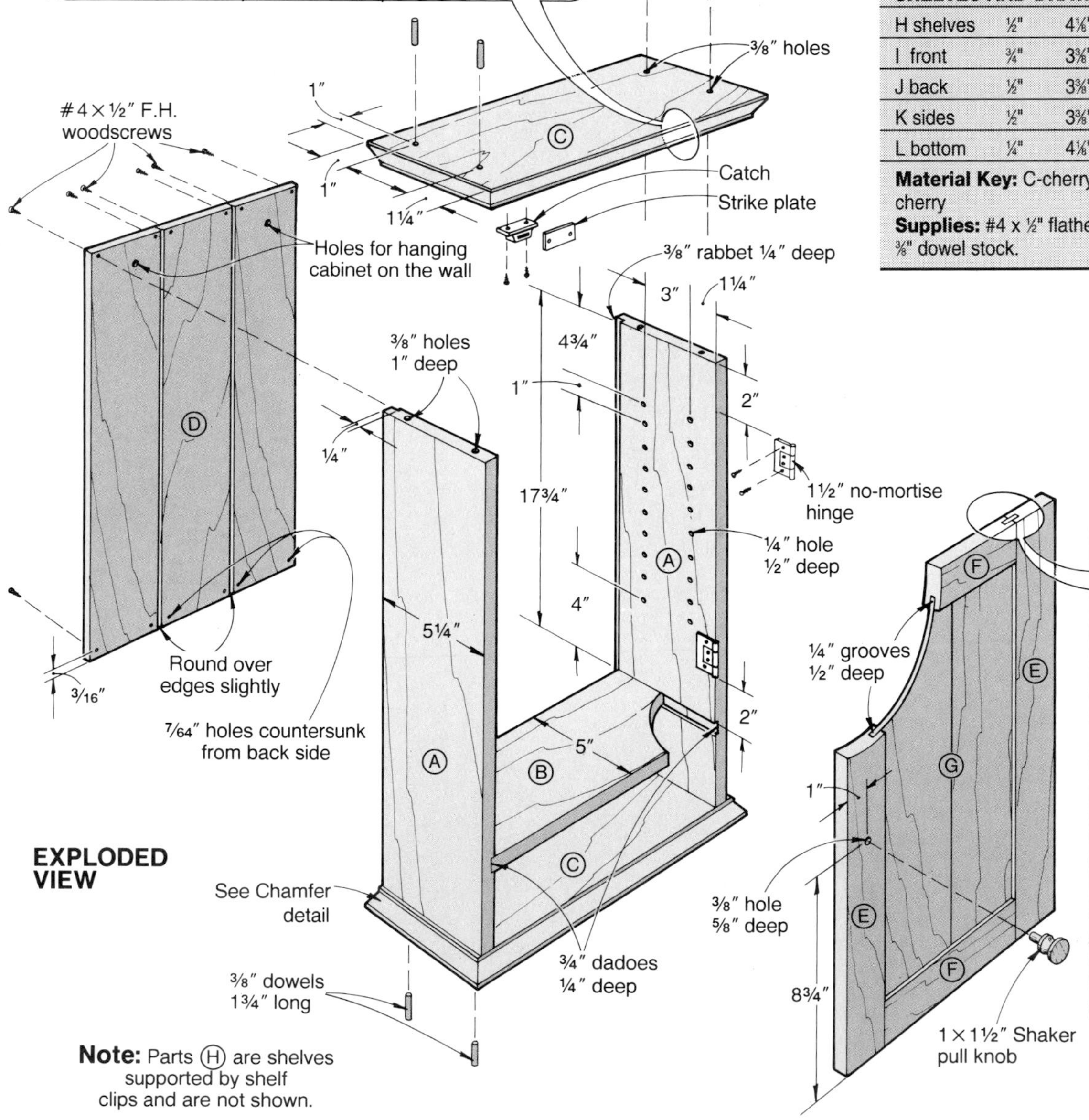
3/8" dowels
1 3/4" long
3/8" holes
1"
1"
1 1/4"
(C)
#4 × 1/2" F.H. woodscrews
Catch
Strike plate
Holes for hanging cabinet on the wall
3/8" rabbet 1/4" deep
3"
1 1/4"
4 3/4"
3/8" holes
1" deep
1"
2"
1/4"
(D)
17 3/4"
1 1/2" no-mortise hinge
1/4" hole
1/2" deep
(A)
4"
5 1/4"
(F)
1/4" grooves
1/2" deep
(E)
3/16"
Round over edges slightly
7/64" holes countersunk from back side
5"
2"
(G)
(A)
(B)
1"
(C)
EXPLODED VIEW
See Chamfer detail
3/8" hole
5/8" deep
(E)
3/4" dadoes
1/4" deep
(F)
3/8" dowels
1 3/4" long
8 3/4"
1 × 1 1/2" Shaker pull knob

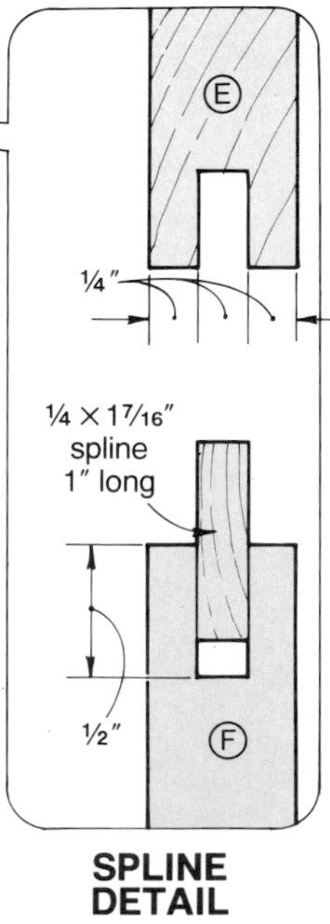
(E)
1/4"
1/4 × 1 7/16" spline
1" long
1/2"
(F)
SPLINE DETAIL

**Note:** Parts (H) are shelves supported by shelf clips and are not shown.

## It's time to add the back

**1.** Cut three pieces of ¼"-thick cherry to 4¹⁄₁₆" wide by 22¾" long for the back panel (D). Sand a slight round-over on the front edges of each piece. (The drawing *below* shows the method we use to resaw thicker stock to size.)

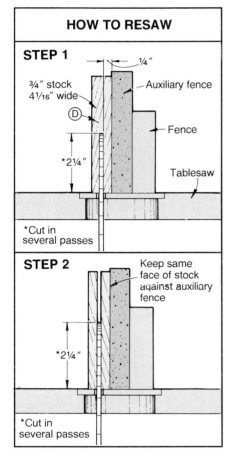

**HOW TO RESAW**

**STEP 1**

¼"

¾" stock
4¹⁄₁₆" wide

Auxiliary fence

D

Fence

*2¼"

Tablesaw

*Cut in
several passes

**STEP 2**

Keep same
face of stock
against auxiliary
fence

*2¼"

*Cut in
several passes

**2.** Rout a ⅜" rabbet ¼" deep along the inside edge of the top and bottom pieces (C) to match the rabbet previously cut in the side pieces. Use a sharp chisel to square the corners where the rabbets meet.

**3.** Lay the cabinet facedown. Position the three back pieces (D) in the rabbeted opening. Drill and countersink holes in the backpanel pieces to the sizes shown on the Exploded View drawing.

## The door comes next

**1.** Cut the door stiles (E) and rails (F) to size. Then, cut two pieces of cherry to 4½x15". Plane or resaw the pieces to ¼" thick for the door panel

(G). Glue and clamp the pieces edge to edge with surfaces and ends flush.

**2.** Cut or rout a ¼" groove ½" deep along one edge of each rail and stile where shown on the Spline detail on the previous page. From ¼" cherry, cut four splines to size.

**3.** Test-fit the door pieces; the panel should be slightly undersized about ¹⁄₁₆" in each direction to allow it to expand *without* splitting the assembled door. Then, glue and clamp the door. Allow the panel to float inside the frame without glue.

**4.** Mark the centerpoint, and drill a hole for the Shaker pull knob.

**5.** Cut the adjustable shelves (H) to size.

## Add the drawer and then the finish

**1.** Cut the drawer front (I), back (J), sides (K), and bottom (L) to sizes listed in the Bill of Materials.

**2.** Cut a ¼" groove ¼" deep ¼" from the bottom edge of the front, back, and side pieces where shown in the drawing *below.*

**3.** Cut ½" rabbets on both ends of the front piece and the back end of each side piece (see the Drawer drawing for particulars).

**4.** Draw diagonal lines from corner to corner to find the center of the drawer front, then drill the mounting hole for the Shaker knob in the drawer front.

**5.** Dry-clamp the pieces and check the fit of the drawer in the opening. Then, glue and clamp the drawer parts.

**6.** Drill a pair of mounting holes through the cabinet back.

**7.** Sand the cabinet, back, door, and drawer. Apply the finish to the cabinet and knobs (we left the cherry natural and brushed on several coats of polyurethane). Add the knobs. Finally, add the magnetic catch and strike plate.

## Buying Guide

• **Hardware.** One ¾"-diam. and one 1"-diam. Shaker pull knobs, one pair of 1½"-long no-mortise hinges, magnetic catch, two 8" pieces of ⅜" cherry dowel. Cabinet kit no. 101WD. For the current prices, contact Cherry Tree Toys, P.O. Box 369, Belmont, OH 43718, or call 800-848-4363 to order.

## Project Tool List

Tablesaw
   Dado blade or dado set
Router
Router table
   ¼" straight bit
   ⅜" rabbet bit
   ¾" chamfer bit
Drill
   Bits: ⁷⁄₆₄", ¼", ⅜"
Finishing sander

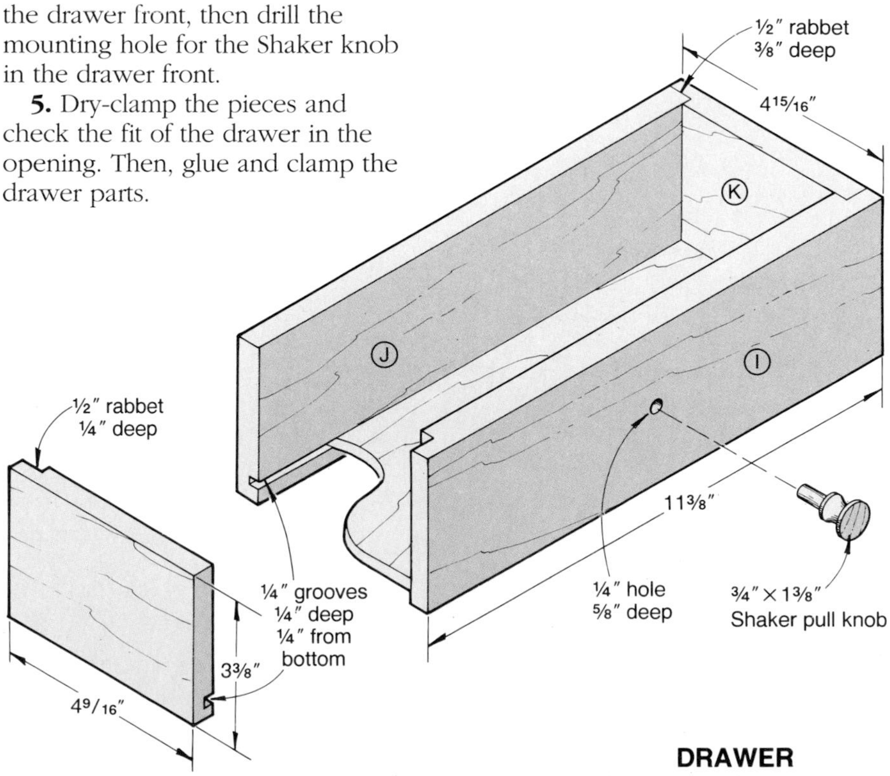

½" rabbet
⅜" deep

4¹⁵⁄₁₆"

K

½" rabbet
¼" deep

J

I

11⅜"

¼" hole
⅝" deep

¾" × 1⅜"
Shaker pull knob

¼" grooves
¼" deep
¼" from
bottom

3⅜"

4⁹⁄₁₆"

**DRAWER**

# EARLY-AMERICAN LADDER SHELF

**C**limb the ladder of decorating success with a shelf tailor-made to fit narrow spaces. We're confident that someone in your house will find just the right collectibles for each rung...er, shelf.

### We'll shape the sides first

**1.** Select a piece of ¾" stock that's at least 9" wide and 96" long. (We chose cherry wood because we wanted a natural-finished hardwood look. If you prefer to paint your shelf, consider pine or poplar stock.) Belt-sand both faces, graduating from 100- to 120- and finally 150-grit sandpaper. Next, square one edge and one end of the piece, and then crosscut a 44" length from it. See the Cutting Diagram *opposite top.*

**2.** Using the dimensions on the Side View drawing *opposite*, mark the locations for the five shelf slots on one face of the 44"-long piece. Next, from scrap ½" particleboard or plywood, make a straightedge to fit over the workpiece as shown *below* to guide the router. (We nailed 1×2" cleats onto the underside to help hold our guide square and aligned with the edges of the board.)

**3.** Chuck a ½" dovetail bit into your router, and adjust it to cut a ⅜"-deep dovetail slot as shown on the Dovetail Slot drawing *above right.* Now, make a test-cut in scrap, and determine how far you need to position the straightedge from the center of the cut.

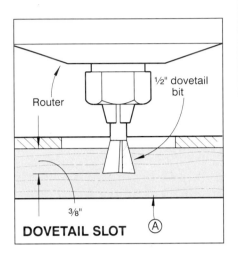

Router    ½" dovetail bit    ⅜"    Ⓐ

**DOVETAIL SLOT**

**4.** To cut the first dovetail slot, position the straightedge you made in Step 2 at the required distance from the dovetail slot centerline, and clamp it in place on the board. (We used scrap pads between the stock and clamps to prevent marring.) Rout the dovetail slot across the width of the piece as shown *above*. Repeat the process to cut the other four dovetail slots.

**5.** Set your tablesaw fence at 4" and rip the two ladder sides (A) from the piece. *continued*

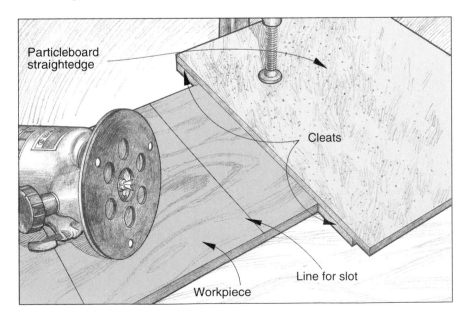

Particleboard straightedge

Cleats

Workpiece

Line for slot

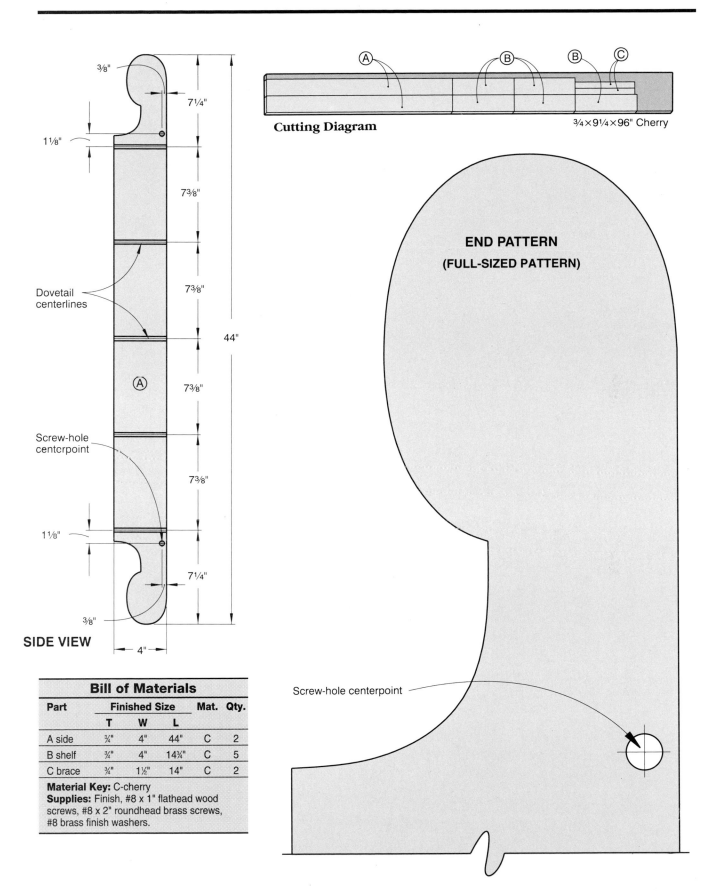

**Cutting Diagram**

¾×9¼×96" Cherry

**END PATTERN**
**(FULL-SIZED PATTERN)**

3/8"

7¼"

1⅛"

7⅜"

Dovetail
centerlines

7⅜"

44"

Ⓐ

7⅜"

Screw-hole
centerpoint

7⅜"

1⅛"

7¼"

3/8"

**SIDE VIEW**

4"

Screw-hole centerpoint

| **Bill of Materials** | | | | | |
|---|---|---|---|---|---|
| **Part** | **Finished Size** | | | **Mat.** | **Qty.** |
| | **T** | **W** | **L** | | |
| A side | ¾" | 4" | 44" | C | 2 |
| B shelf | ¾" | 4" | 14¾" | C | 5 |
| C brace | ¾" | 1½" | 14" | C | 2 |

**Material Key:** C-cherry
**Supplies:** Finish, #8 x 1" flathead wood
screws, #8 x 2" roundhead brass screws,
#8 brass finish washers.

**41**

# EARLY-AMERICAN LADDER SHELF

*continued*

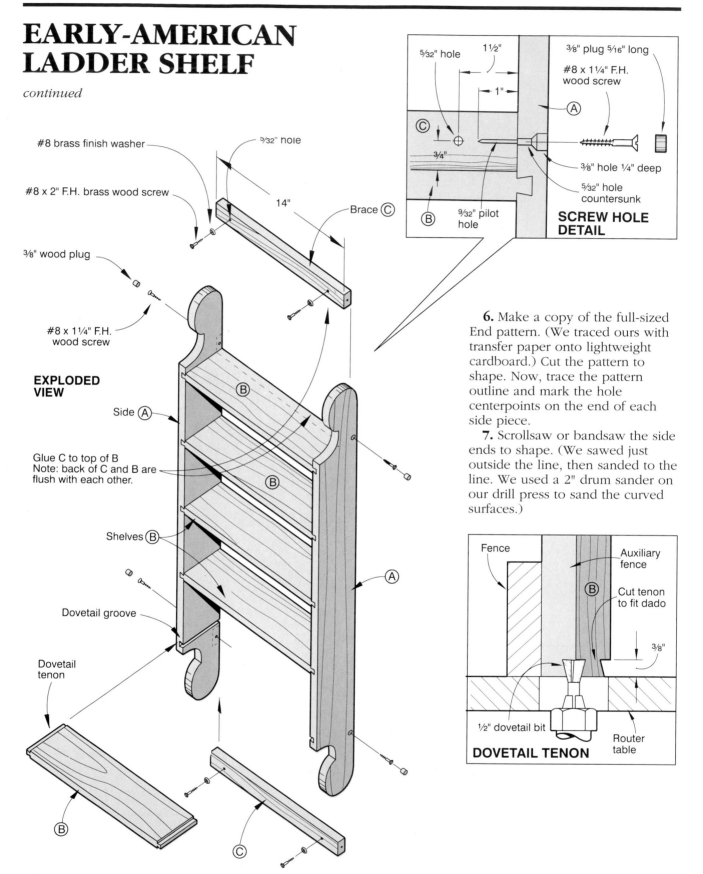

#8 brass finish washer

#8 x 2" F.H. brass wood screw

⁹⁄₃₂" hole

14"

Brace Ⓒ

³⁄₈" wood plug

#8 x 1¼" F.H. wood screw

**EXPLODED VIEW**

Side Ⓐ

Glue C to top of B
Note: back of C and B are flush with each other.

Shelves Ⓑ

Dovetail groove

Dovetail tenon

Ⓑ

Ⓑ

Ⓑ

Ⓐ

Ⓐ

Ⓒ

Ⓑ

**SCREW HOLE DETAIL**

⁵⁄₃₂" hole

1½"

1"

³⁄₈" plug ⁵⁄₁₆" long

#8 x 1¼" F.H. wood screw

Ⓐ

Ⓒ

³⁄₄"

Ⓑ

⁹⁄₃₂" pilot hole

³⁄₈" hole ¼" deep

⁵⁄₃₂" hole countersunk

**6.** Make a copy of the full-sized End pattern. (We traced ours with transfer paper onto lightweight cardboard.) Cut the pattern to shape. Now, trace the pattern outline and mark the hole centerpoints on the end of each side piece.

**7.** Scrollsaw or bandsaw the side ends to shape. (We sawed just outside the line, then sanded to the line. We used a 2" drum sander on our drill press to sand the curved surfaces.)

Fence

Auxiliary fence

Ⓑ

Cut tenon to fit dado

³⁄₈"

½" dovetail bit

Router table

**DOVETAIL TENON**

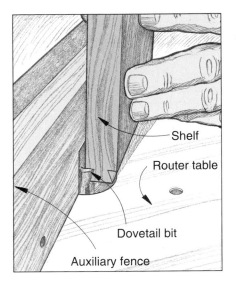

Shelf

Router table

Dovetail bit

Auxiliary fence

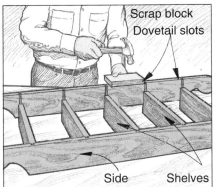

Scrap block

Dovetail slots

Side          Shelves

## Let's make the shelves next

**1.** From the remaining ¾" cherry, rip and crosscut five pieces to 4½x14¾" for the shelves (B).

**2.** Finish-sand the edges. Next, mount your router to your router table. Set up the bit and fence to cut a dovetail tenon on the ends of each shelf as shown on the Dovetail Tenon drawing *opposite*. Size the tenon to fit snugly in the dovetail slots you cut into the sides. (We first tested the router setup on same-sized scrap material.) Now, rout the dovetail tenons on the ends of each shelf as shown here. Finally, trim the shelves to 4" wide.

*Note:* If you'd like to display plates on shelf, rout or dado ⅜ x ¼" grooves to the tops of the shelves at this time. Adjust spacing between the edge and groove to fit the size of plates you'll display.

**3.** Locate the centerpoints for the screw holes you marked on the ends of each side earlier. Drill and counterbore these four holes as shown on the Screw Hole detail associated with the Exploded View drawing *opposite*.

**4.** Working first on one side, apply yellow woodworker's glue in the dovetail slots, and then insert the dovetail tenon of each shelf in a slot. Next, apply glue in the slots of the second side, and start the shelf tenons in the slots. Now, as shown *lower left*, drive that side onto the shelf tenons. Align the shelves and sides. Clamp lightly and wipe off glue squeeze-out with a damp cloth. Check your assembly for square and adjust the clamps if necessary.

**5.** Rip and crosscut two ¾x1½" cherry pieces for the backs (C) to fit between the sides. Locate and drill the ⁵⁄₃₂"-mounting holes near the ends of both where shown on the Screw Hole detail. Finish-sand the pieces. Next, glue and screw both backs to the shelf where shown on the Exploded View, using #8x1½" flathead wood screws. Wipe off glue squeeze-out with a damp cloth. Using a ⅜" plug cutter, cut four plugs from cherry scrap. Glue one into each screw hole. Using 180-grit sandpaper, sand the plugs flush with the sides. Now, finish-sand the entire piece.

## The final steps

**1.** Apply the finish of your choice. (We wanted a natural cherry look, so we left the wood unstained. First, we applied two coats of water-based sanding sealer, and then two coats of water-based satin lacquer, sanding with 220-grit sandpaper after each coat dried thoroughly.)

**2.** Attach the shelf to your wall as detailed on the Exploded View drawing with #8x2" roundhead brass screws and brass finish washers. If possible, position the shelf so you can drive at least one pair of screws into wall studs. If you can't, use wall anchors.

## Project Tool List
Tablesaw
Bandsaw
Belt sander
Router
   Router table
   ½" dovetail bit
Drill
   Bits: ⁹⁄₆₄", ⁵⁄₃₂", ⅜"
⅜" plug cutter
Finishing sander

*Note: We built this project using the tools listed. You may be able to substitute other tools and equipment for listed items you don't have. You'll also need various common hand tools and clamps to complete the project.*

# THE SHAKER OVAL CARRIER

**O**n a summer vacation, Jim Downing, our design editor, visited the Hancock Shaker Village near Pittsfield, Massachusetts. At the woodshop, craftsman Cliff Myers invited Jim to join him in making a traditional Shaker carrier. After trying the techniques in our own shop, we're inviting you to construct a bit of history for yourself.

*Note: You'll need some thin stock for the carrier and handle. You can plane or resaw thicker stock to size, or see our source listed in the Buying Guide for this project.*

### Construct the band form, pipe support, and two shapers

**1.** Cut four pieces of ¾"-thick stock to 6x9" (two pieces of 2x8 also would work). Glue and clamp the pieces with the ends and edges flush.

**2.** Transfer the full-sized band-form pattern from the opposite page to the top piece of stock. Bandsaw the form to shape. Sand the form edges.

**3.** Mark the start-point reference line on the top surface of the form where shown on the full-sized patterns drawing.

**4.** Refer to the Pipe Support drawing *opposite* to build the support. You'll use this and a pipe clamp later to clinch the tacks that hold the carrier together.

**5.** Transfer the shaper outline from the full-sized pattern drawing to two pieces of ¾" stock that measure 6x9". Tilt your bandsaw table 10° from horizontal. Bandsaw the two shapers to shape, cutting just *outside* the marked line (the entire line should still be visible when you're done cutting). Drill two 1" holes in each shaper where shown on the drawing titled Shaping the Carrier Band.

### The carrier band comes next

**1.** Cut a piece of 5/64" (.075") thick cherry to 3x27". See the Buying Guide for our source of thin cherry or plane your own to size. (The Shakers also used maple and ash.)

**2.** Transfer the full-sized finger pattern and hole locations to one end of the band (see the full-sized pattern for reference). Drill twelve 1/16" holes through the band where marked.

**3.** On the end opposite the fingers, sand a 1½"-long taper. See the drawing on page 46 for reference.

**4.** Bandsaw the fingers to shape. Using a utility or hobby knife and the full-sized band pattern for reference, bevel-cut the edges and ends of each finger. (We followed the Shaker style of beveling the insides of the fingers at about 20° and reducing the bevel to 10° near the end of the fingers.) Now, come back and finish forming the beveled V where the 20° cuts meet. Next, bevel-cut the ends of the fingers.

**5.** Soak the band in hot water for 25 minutes (we did this in a plastic wallpaper water tray; a bathtub also would work). Drain the water and immediately pour boiling water over the band and soak it for one minute. Working quickly now, remove the band from the water and wrap it snugly around the form. Position the band so that the tapered end sits directly under the start-point reference line on the

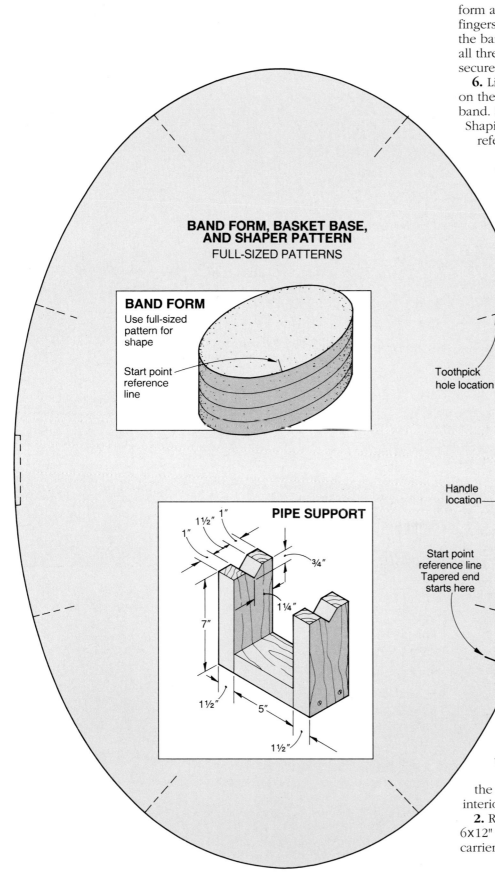

## BAND FORM, BASKET BASE, AND SHAPER PATTERN
### FULL-SIZED PATTERNS

**BAND FORM**

Use full-sized pattern for shape

Start point reference line

Toothpick hole location

Handle location

Start point reference line Tapered end starts here

**PIPE SUPPORT**

1½"
1"
1"
¾"
1¼"
7"
1½"
5"
1½"

---

form and the beveled edges on the fingers face out. To avoid splitting the band between the fingers, hold all three fingers until the tacks are secured in the following steps.

**6.** Lightly mark a reference line on the top-lapped edges of the band. See the drawing titled Shaping the Carrier Band for reference.

**7.** Insert a pipe clamp through the oval band, and place the pipe on the support. Lightly tighten the clamp to hold it to the support.

**8.** Hold the band with one hand so the marked lines on the top edges align and the band edges are flush. Position the ¹⁄₁₆" holes in the band directly over the pipe. Drive #1½ copper tacks through the holes and against the pipe as shown in the photo on page 47. The end of the tack will clinch against the pipe. Don't drive the tacks at an angle; they won't clinch properly and will cause the band to fit loosely.

**9.** As shown on the drawing titled Shaping the Carrier Handle, slip a shaper into each end of the band and let the band dry and cool on the shapers overnight.

### Now, shape and install the carrier base

**1.** Remove the shapers from the band, and sand the band interior.

**2.** Resaw or plane a piece of 6x12" pine to ¼" thick for the carrier base. Transfer the full-sized
*continued*

# THE SHAKER OVAL CARRIER

*continued*

base pattern to the pine. Bandsaw the base to shape, cutting about ⅛" *outside* the marked line.

**3.** Tilt the table on your disc sander 4° from horizontal (or, use a belt sander on a conversion stand). Now, bevel-sand to the line until the base fits snugly into the band and until the bottom edge of the band is flush with the bottom edge of the base.

**4.** If any small gaps exist on the bottom surface of the carrier between the band and base, fill with glue and wipe off the excess. Immediately sand the bottom surface to load the glue-filled crevice with sawdust and flush the edge of the band with that of the base.

**5.** Drill ⁵⁄₆₄" holes through the band and ½" into the base (see the full-sized pattern drawing for hole locations and the Toothpick Hole detail at *right* for reference).

Tap a round toothpick through the hole in the band and into the base. Trim the end of the toothpick and sand it flush with the outside surface of the band.

### A tapered handle adds 'that Shaker look'

**1.** Cut a piece of ⅛" cherry to ¾" wide by 18½" long for the handle. Transfer the full-sized handle pattern and hole locations to both ends of the handle strip. Bandsaw the four curves to shape. Using the rounded end of a belt sander or a drum sander, lightly sand the bandsawed contours. Drill three ¹⁄₁₆" holes through each end of the handle where marked.

**2.** Follow the same soaking method used for the band. Remove the band from the water, and immediately center and wrap it over one end of the band form.

**3.** Position the handle in the basket. Apply a small bead of glue to the mating surfaces of the handle, and then drive ⁷⁄₁₆"-long copper tacks from the inside

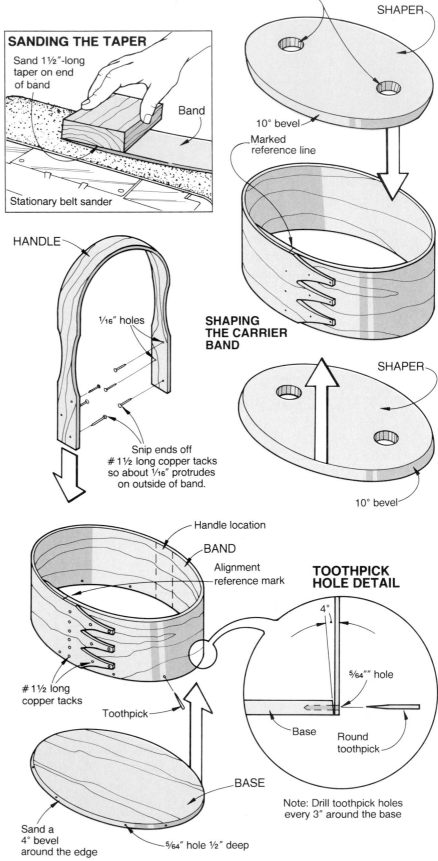

**SANDING THE TAPER**

Sand 1½"-long taper on end of band

Band

Stationary belt sander

1" holes

SHAPER

10° bevel

Marked reference line

HANDLE

¹⁄₁₆" holes

Snip ends off # 1½ long copper tacks so about ¹⁄₁₆" protrudes on outside of band.

**SHAPING THE CARRIER BAND**

SHAPER

10° bevel

Handle location

BAND

Alignment reference mark

# 1½ long copper tacks

Toothpick

BASE

Sand a 4° bevel around the edge

⁵⁄₆₄" hole ½" deep

**TOOTHPICK HOLE DETAIL**

4°

⁵⁄₆₄" hole

Base

Round toothpick

Note: Drill toothpick holes every 3" around the base

through the handle and band and against the pipe on the support to fasten the handle to the carrier. See the Exploded View drawing for the sizes of tacks to use. For the tacks going through the back of the carrier, drive the tacks through the handle and band, snip ⅛" off the ends, and then drive them against the pipe to clinch the ends.

**4.** Sand and finish the carrier. The Shakers used milk paints, stains, and clear finishes.

### Buying Guide
• **Band stock and tacks.**
.075"-thick cherry 3x27" (enough for one band); ⅛"-thick cherry ⅞"x18½" (enough for one handle); ¼"-thick quarter-sawn cherry 6x9" (enough for one bottom board). Enough #1½ copper tacks (⁷⁄₃₂" long), #1½ long copper tacks (⁷⁄₁₆" long), and wood pegs for one carrier. For the current price, contact John Wilson, 500 East Broadway, Charlotte, MI 48813, or call 517-543-5325 to order.

### Project Tool List
Tablesaw
Bandsaw
Drill
   Bits: ¹⁄₁₆", ⁵⁄₆₄", 1"
Disc sander
Belt sander
Finishing sander

**Note:** *We built this project using the tools listed. You may be able to substitute other tools and equipment for listed items you don't have. You'll also need various common hand tools and clamps to complete the project.*

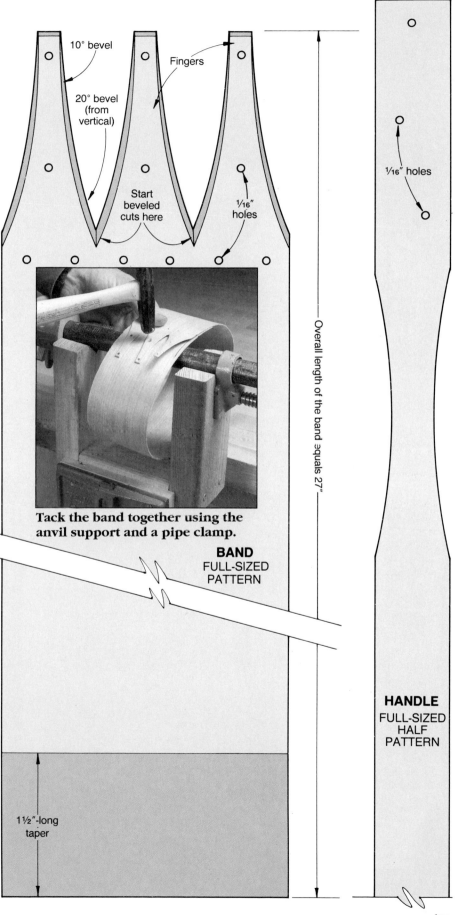

**Tack the band together using the anvil support and a pipe clamp.**

10° bevel

20° bevel (from vertical)

Fingers

Start beveled cuts here

¹⁄₁₆" holes

¹⁄₁₆" holes

Overall length of the band equals 27"

**BAND**
FULL-SIZED PATTERN

**HANDLE**
FULL-SIZED HALF PATTERN

1½"-long taper

# ODDS 'N' ENDS COUNTRY SHADOW BOX

**F**anciers of small collectibles, at last you have the perfect project for showcasing thimbles and other small items. Then, add our counted cross-stitch design for a center highlight.

*Note: See page 50 for the stitchwork pattern we used and the Exploded View drawing for the dimensions of the ¼"-thick piece used to back the stitchwork.*

To make the side pieces (A), cut a piece 12⅞" long by 3⅝" wide from ¼" stock (plane or resaw thicker stock). Using a try square and the dimensions on the Exploded View drawing, mark the location of the ¼" dadoes on the stock. Now, cut or rout ¼" dadoes ⅛" deep across the piece where marked. Rip two 1 ½"-wide side pieces (A) from the 3⅝"-wide dadoed piece.

## DADO DETAIL

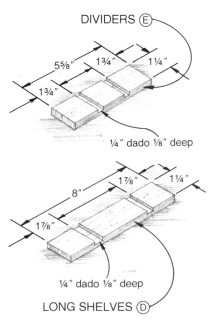

DIVIDERS Ⓔ

5⅝"    1¾"    1¼"

1¾"

¼" dado ⅛" deep

8"    1⅞"    1¼"

1⅞"

¼" dado ⅛" deep

LONG SHELVES Ⓓ

**EXPLODED VIEW**

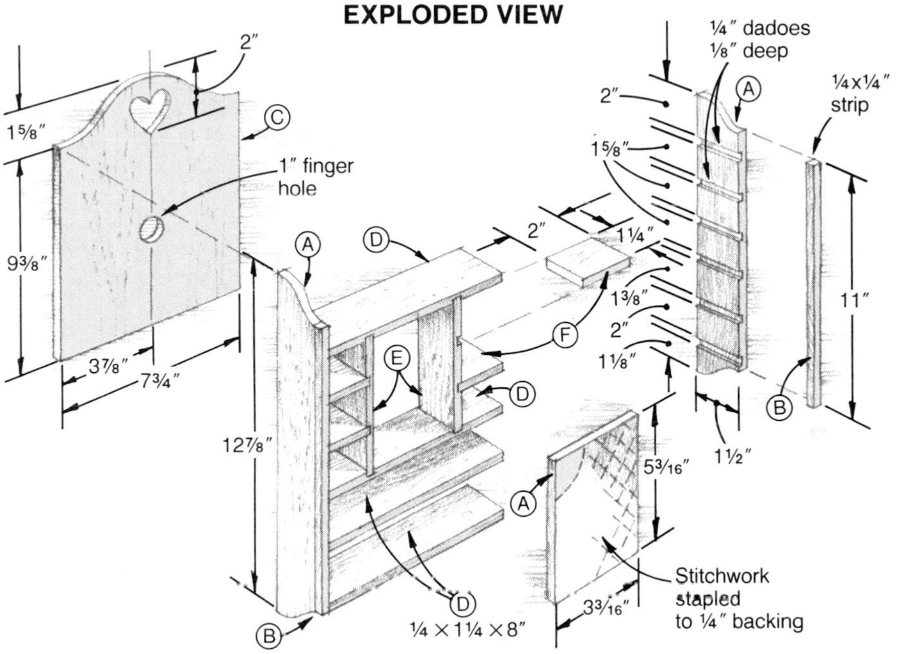

2"
1⅝"
9⅜"
C
1" finger hole
3⅞"
7¾"
A
D
12⅞"
E
D
F
2"
1¼"
A
D
B
¼ × 1¼ × 8"
¼" dadoes ⅛" deep
2"
1⅝"
1⅜"
2"
1⅛"
A
¼x¼" strip
11"
B
1½"
5³⁄₁₆"
3³⁄₁₆"
Stitchwork stapled to ¼" backing


**DRAWER**

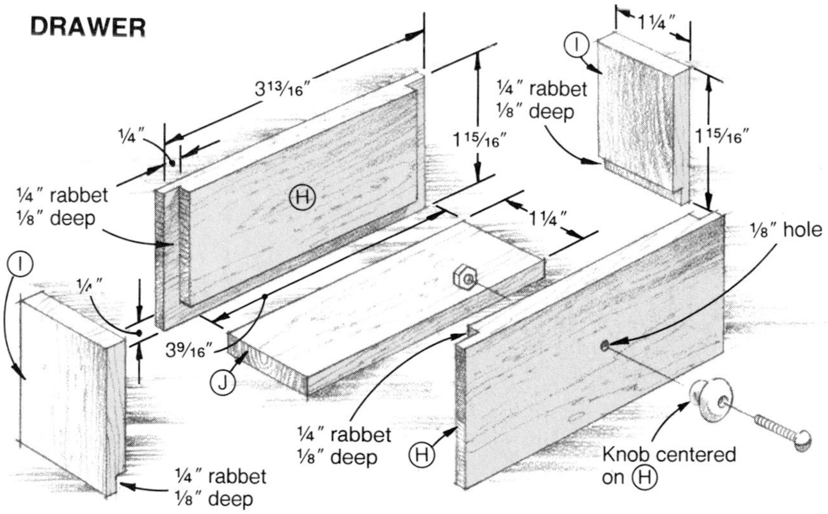

3¹³⁄₁₆"
¼"
¼" rabbet ⅛" deep
H
I
¼"
3⁹⁄₁₆"
J
¼" rabbet ⅛" deep
1¹⁵⁄₁₆"
¼" rabbet ⅛" deep
1¼"
I
1¼"
1¹⁵⁄₁₆"
⅛" hole
¼" rabbet ⅛" deep
H
Knob centered on H


Cut two pieces of ¼" stock to ¼" wide by 12⅞" long for the facing strips (B). With the surfaces and ends flush, glue and clamp a strip to the front of each side (A).

Transfer the full-sized top and bottom pattern shown on page 50 to the cabinet sides (A, B). Using a scrollsaw or bandsaw, cut the top and bottom of each cabinet side to shape.

From ¼" stock, cut the two back pieces to 3⅞" wide by 11" long for the backboard (C). Transfer the heart outline to each of the 3⅞"-wide pieces. Then, cut the pieces to shape, and glue and clamp them edge to edge.

Transfer the Backboard Top pattern to the backboard, and cut to shape. Drill a 1" finger hole through the backboard. The hole allows you to easily remove the stitchwork without prying.

Cut the four long shelves (D) and the two dividers (E) to the sizes shown in the Dado detail. Mark the dado locations on two of the shelves and both dividers where dimensioned on the detail. Cut or rout the dadoes. Cut the four short shelves (F) to size. Dryclamp the assembly to check the fit of all the pieces. Trim if necessary. Then, glue and clamp the assembly, checking for square. Measure the opening, and cut the stitchwork backing (G) to size minus 1/16" in length and width.

Using the Drawer drawing for reference, cut pieces H, I, J to size. Cut ¼" rabbets ⅛" deep where shown. Glue and clamp each drawer. Drill a ⅛" hole in the center of each drawer front.

Brush on the desired color of paint. (For our country antique look, we applied a medium blue paint, followed by a light blue. Next, we sanded the edges to make the project appear worn. Finally, we speckled the project the dark navy blue.)

*continued*

# ODDS 'N' ENDS COUNTRY SHADOW BOX
*continued*

Attach the knobs. With the quilt batting in place, stretch the stitch-work around the backing piece and staple it in place. Slide the stitch-work/backing in place, and hang the project where it's sure to be noticed.

**Project Tool List**
Tablesaw
   Dado blade or dado set
Bandsaw or scrollsaw
Drill
   Bits: ⅛", 1"
Finishing sander

*Note:* *We built this project using the tools listed. You may be able to substitute other tools and equipment for listed items you don't have. You'll also need various common hand tools and clamps to complete the project.*

**Cut a piece of 14-count marine blue aida to 5¼X7⅜". This allows an inch overhang on all edges. Center and stitch the full-sized pattern shown at right to the fabric. We used white embroidery floss.**

## FULL-SIZED PATTERNS

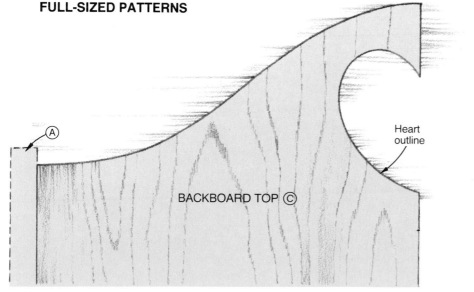

Heart outline

BACKBOARD TOP Ⓒ

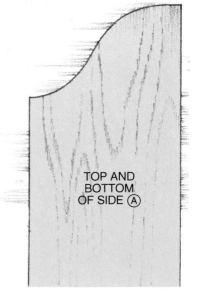

TOP AND BOTTOM OF SIDE Ⓐ

# SIMPLY STATED SHAKER WALL CLOCK

Like wall clocks built by the Shakers in the early 19th century, our version features clean, unadorned design lines. Although the Shakers frowned upon watches, wall clocks abounded. Today, collectors seek out the originals and pay dearly for them.

**Start with the cherry clock case**

**1.** From ¾"-thick cherry, cut the sides (A) and the interior top and bottom (B) to the sizes listed in the Bill of Materials.

**2.** Cut or rout a ¾" rabbet ¼" deep across the ends and a ¼" rabbet ½" deep along back inside edge of both side pieces where shown on the Exploded View drawing. Then, form a ¼" rabbet ½" deep along the back edge of the top and bottom interior pieces.

**3.** Glue and clamp the clock assembly (A, B), checking for square. Remove excess glue with a damp cloth.

**4.** Cut the exterior top and bottom pieces (C) to size.

**5.** Fit your table-mounted router with an edge-rounding bit (we used a Craftsman 9GT26337) and fence. Raise the bit where shown on the Routing detail accompanying the Exploded View drawing on page 53. Using the same detail for reference, position the fence and bit where shown. (We test-cut ¾" scrap stock first to verify that the routed cut was centered along the edge of the stock.)

*continued*

To build your own Shaker-style classic, use a solid panel in the door bottom. Or, for a more modern appearance and a view of the pendulum (something considered showy and therefore an unusual Shaker practice), try a glass insert.

# SIMPLY STATED SHAKER WALL CLOCK
*continued*

**6.** Rout the front and side edges (not the back edge) of the exterior top and bottom pieces (C). When making the last cut (across the grain), use a piece of scrap stock to reduce splintering as shown on the drawing *below*.

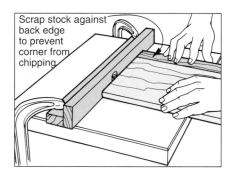

Scrap stock against back edge to prevent corner from chipping

**7.** Mark the ¾x4" notch on the back edge of the top exterior part (C) where shown on the Exploded View drawing. With a bandsaw or scrollsaw, cut the marked notch to shape.

### It's time to add the cleats, clock face, support, and back

**1.** Cut the three cleats (D) to size. Glue and clamp them to the inside of the case where shown on the Exploded View drawing.

**2.** Cut the bottom cleat (E) and the clock-face panel (F) to size. Glue the bottom cleat to the front bottom edge of the clock-face panel, with the ends and bottom edges flush, where shown on the Exploded View drawing.

**3.** Place the clock face on the clock-face panel (F). Trace the shaft hole and four screw mounting holes from the clock-face openings onto the plywood panel. Remove the clock face and drill a ⅜" shaft hole where marked. Then, drill four ¹⁄₁₆" screw holes where marked.

**4.** Measure the opening and cut the back panel (G) to size from ¼" cherry plywood.

**5.** Transfer the full-sized half-round clock-support (H) outline

and the three hole centerpoints to ¾" cherry. Bore a 1" hole where marked. Next, drill and countersink a pair of ⁵⁄₃₂" shank holes where marked.

**6.** Cut the clock support to shape. Sand the radiused edge smooth to remove the saw marks.

**7.** Cut the clock support to shape. Glue the clock support into the notch in the exterior top piece (C). Then, using the previously drilled shank holes in the notch as guides, drill a pair of ⁷⁄₆₄" pilot holes ¾" deep into the top piece (C). Drill the same sized mounting hole through the top interior piece (B) and into the support where shown on the Exploded View drawing and accompanying the Clock Support Mounting detail. Drive a trio of #8x1½" wood screws to further secure the clock support to the clock assembly.

### Now, for the door

**1.** Cut the door stiles (I), top and bottom rails (J), and center rail (K) to size.

**2.** Fit your tablesaw with a ¼" dado set and cut a ¼" groove ⅜" deep centered along *one* edge of parts I and J and *both* edges of the center rail (K) as shown in the photo at *right*. (Note that we used a feather board to keep the pieces firmly against the fence. We also test-cut scrap first to verify that the groove was accurately centered along the edge.)

**3.** As shown in the photo *opposite*, cut a ¼" tenon ⅜" long across the ends of the three rails (J, K). See the Tenon detail *opposite* for dimensions.

**4.** If you want to install the solid cherry panel (L) instead of a glass insert, cut two 5½"x19" pieces of ½" stock (we planed ¾" stock to ½" thick). Edge-join the ½"-thick pieces, checking that the surfaces and ends are flush. Later, trim both ends and one edge to cut the edge-joined cherry panel to finished size. Sand the panel. Cut or rout a ⅜" rabbet ¼" deep along all front edges

of the panel where shown on the Door drawing *opposite*.

**5.** Glue and clamp the door pieces—including the door panel if you intend to use it—checking for square. See the Panel detail on page 54 for reference.

**6.** Fit your router with a ⅜" rabbeting bit. If you plan to fit both the upper and lower openings with glass, rout along the back inside edge of both openings in the door. See the Glass and Panel details accompanying the Door drawing and the Lower Glass Panel Installation drawings for reference.

*continued*

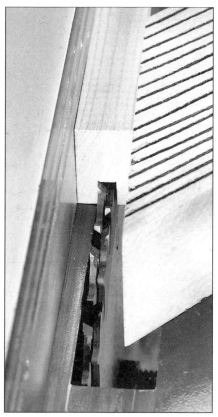

**Cut a ¼" groove ⅜" deep centered along the door parts. Clamp a feather board securely to your saw table to hold the pieces firmly against the fence.**

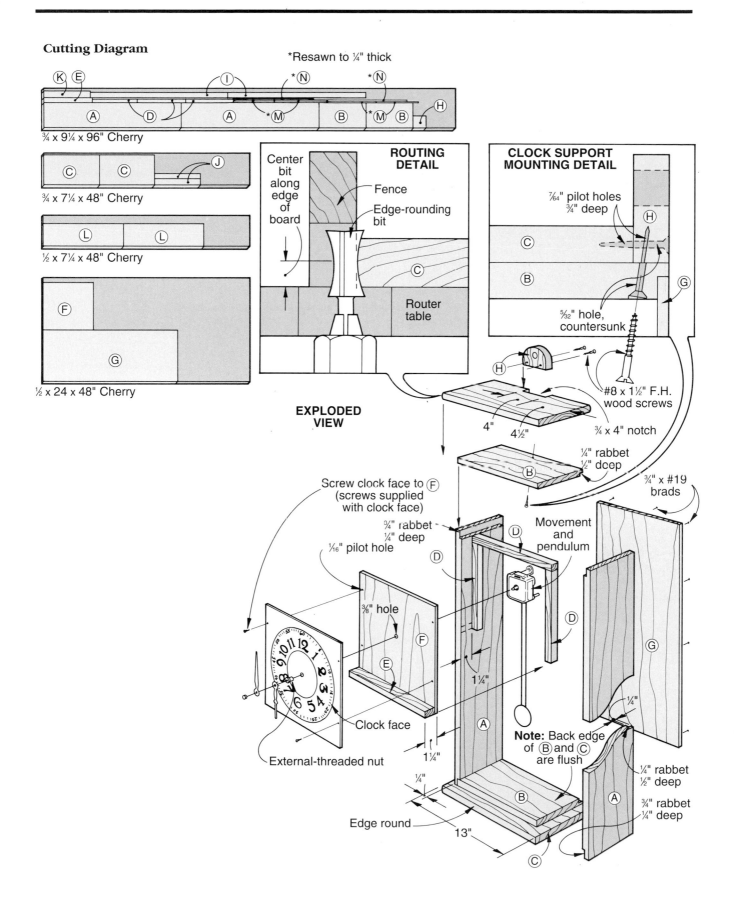

**Cut a ¼" tenon ⅜" long across the ends of the rails. Clamp a stop to the miter-gauge fence for consistent tenon lengths.**

| Part | Finished Size | | | Mat. | Qty. |
|---|---|---|---|---|---|
| | T | W | L | | |
| **CLOCK CASE** | | | | | |
| A sides | ¾" | 6" | 32" | C | 2 |
| B top & bottom | ¾" | 6" | 11½" | C | 2 |
| C top & bottom | ¾" | 7⅛" | 13" | C | 2 |
| D cleats | ¾" | ¾" | 11" | C | 3 |
| E cleat | ¾" | 1" | 11" | C | 1 |
| F panel | ¼" | 11" | 11¾" | CP | 1 |
| G back panel | ¼" | 12" | 31½" | CP | 1 |
| H support | ¾" | 4" | 2¾" | C | 1 |
| **DOOR** | | | | | |
| I stiles | ¾" | 1¼" | 31⅞" | C | 2 |
| J rails | ¾" | 1¼" | 10¾" | C | 2 |
| K center rail | ¾" | 1½" | 10¾" | C | 1 |
| L panel | ½" | 10⅝" | 18⁹⁄₁₆" | EC | 1 |
| M stops | ¼" | ¼" | 10¾" | C | 4 |
| N stops | ¼" | ¼" | 18⅝" | C | 2 |

**Material Key:** C—cherry, CP—cherry plywood, EC—edge-joined cherry

**Supplies:** ½" x #19 brads, ¾" x #19 brads, #8 x 1½" flathead wood screws, ⅛" x 10¹¹⁄₁₆" x 10¹¹⁄₁₆" glass, clear finish.

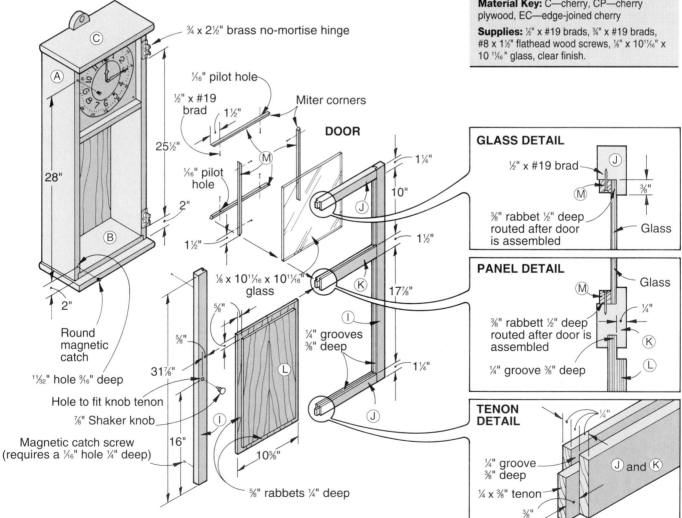

Bill of Materials

# SIMPLY STATED SHAKER WALL CLOCK

*continued*

**7.** Cut four glass stops (M) to size, miter-cutting the ends for the top opening. Cut the bottom opening glass stops (M, N) if required. Snip the head off a ½"x#19 brad, chuck the brad into your portable electric drill, and use the brad as a bit to drill pilot holes through the glass stops ½" in from the ends where shown on the Door drawing.

**8.** Drill the holes for the knob and magnetic catches. Glue the knob in place.

### Add the finish, hardware, and movement

**1.** Stain and/or finish the case, door, back panel, knob, and glass stops as desired. (We left ours unstained and applied three coats of satin polyurethane.)

**2.** Install the glass and the glass stops. See the Glass detail accompanying the Door drawing for reference. Screw the clock face to the plywood panel (F).

**3.** Attach the hinges to the front edge of the right-hand side piece (A) where shown on the Door drawing. Then, fasten the hinges to the door stile. When positioning the door for attaching the hinges, allow ¹⁄₁₆" gap between the clock case and the top and bottom of the door.

**4.** Insert the magnetic catches into the previously drilled holes, and mark their mating locations on the back face of the door stile. Drill a pair of mounting holes in the back face of the door, and drive the screws, which act as strike plates.

**5.** Brad the back panel (G) into the rabbet in the clock back.

**6.** Stick the clock shaft through the hole in the plywood panel, and fasten the movement (minus the pendulum) to the panel and clock-face with the external-threaded nut. Add the hands to the clock shaft. Hang the clock on the wall (or a Shaker peg as shown in the opening photograph). Add the pendulum and battery, and set the time.

### Buying Guide

•**Shaker clock kit.** Quartz pendulum movement, hands and dial, ⅞" Shaker peg, two ¾ x 2½" brass no-mortise hinges, two ⁵⁄₁₆" catches. For the current price, contact Meisel Hardware Specialties, PO Box 70, Mound, MN 55364-0070, or call 800-441-9870.

### Project Tool List

Tablesaw
   Dado blade or dado set
Bandsaw or scrollsaw
Router
   Router table
   Edge-rounding bit
   ¼" rabbeting bit
   ⅜" rabbeting bit
Drill
   Bits: ¹⁄₁₆", ⁷⁄₆₄", ⁵⁄₃₂", ¹¹⁄₃₂", ⅜", 1"
Disc or belt sander
Finishing sander

***Note:*** *We built this project using the tools listed. You may be able to substitute other tools and equipment for listed items you don't have. You'll also need various common hand tools and clamps to complete the project.*

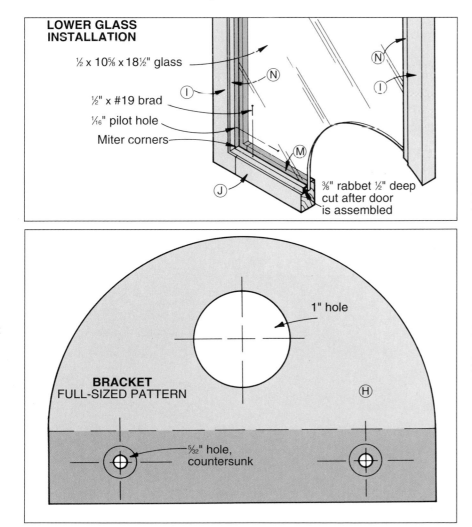

**LOWER GLASS INSTALLATION**
½ x 10⅝ x 18½" glass
½" x #19 brad
¹⁄₁₆" pilot hole
Miter corners
⅜" rabbet ½" deep cut after door is assembled

**BRACKET FULL-SIZED PATTERN**
1" hole
⁵⁄₃₂" hole, countersunk

# COUNTRY-COLORS QUILT STAND

When spring turns to summer, you may be wondering where to store those winter quilts or colorful blankets. They're often too beautiful to hide in a drawer. Our quilt stand provides the perfect answer. Designed to hold one quilt or a couple, it's handsome and easy to build.

**Note:** *You'll need two 1¹⁄₁₆x4x36" hardwood boards, two more at 1¹⁄₁₆x3x18", and one at 1¹⁄₁₆x4½x24" to build the stand. (We used maple.) Make the quilt rods from two 1x28½" dowels and four 2" hardwood balls.*

Trace the full-sized pattern, *opposite* page, onto cardboard and cut it out. With this template, mark the profile on one end of each 36"-long board for the uprights (A). See the Exploded View drawing for reference.

Lay out the stretcher (B) on the 24"-long piece, and the legs (C) on the 18"-long pieces, following the dimensions on the radiused drawings *below* and *opposite*. Now, bandsaw the stretcher, legs, and upright tops. With your tablesaw, crosscut the uprights to 33".

Tilt your drill-press table to 30°, and drill ½" holes 1½" deep centered on the edges of the uprights where shown. With the table at 0° (perpendicular to the bit), bore ¾" holes ⅝" deep at the screw-hole locations on the outer face of the uprights and the underside of the legs. Then, with a ⁹⁄₃₂" bit, drill the screw holes through the uprights and legs.

Now, clamp each leg to its upright. Chuck the ⁹⁄₃₂" bit into a hand drill to mark a center on the upright at each hole. Clamp the stretcher to the uprights, and mark as above. Drill a ³⁄₁₆" hole at each mark, 1½" into the uprights and 2½" into the stretcher.

Assemble the legs, uprights, and stretcher with woodworker's glue and ¼"x3" lag screws with washers. Cover the screw heads in the uprights with wooden buttons.

Cut twelve 4" lengths of ½" dowel. Chuck each into the drill press about 1" deep, and then round over the end using 80-grit sandpaper on a sanding block. Finish-sand with 120-grit sandpaper. Glue the dowels, rounded ends out, into the angled holes on the uprights.

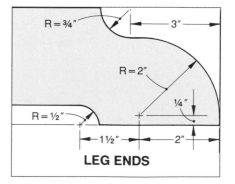

**LEG ENDS**

Cut two 1" dowels to 28½" for the quilt rods. To glue a 2"-diameter wooden ball to each end of each rod, bore a 1" hole ¾" deep into each ball. To do so, clamp a piece of scrapwood 2x4x6" to the drill-press table, and bore a 1½" hole 1" deep into it. Without moving the block, change to a 1" bit. Place the wooden ball into the hole, and grip with a handscrew clamp to bore the hole.

Sand, and apply a clear finish. (We sprayed on clear lacquer, rubbing with 0000 steel wool between coats.)

**Project Tool List**
Tablesaw
Bandsaw
Drill
Drill press
    Bits: ³⁄₁₆", ⁹⁄₃₂", ½", ¾", 1", 1½"
Finishing sander

**Note:** *We built this project using the tools listed. You may be able to substitute other tools and equipment for listed items you don't have. You'll also need various common hand tools and clamps to complete the project.*

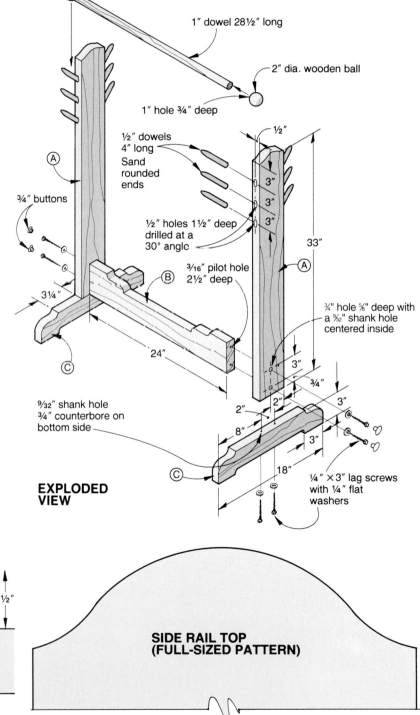

1" dowel 28½" long

2" dia. wooden ball

1" hole ¾" deep

½" dowels 4" long Sand rounded ends

¾" buttons

½" holes 1½" deep drilled at a 30° angle

³⁄₁₆" pilot hole 2½" deep

3"
3"
3"

33"

¾" hole ⅝" deep with a ⁹⁄₃₂" shank hole centered inside

3¼"

24"

½"

¾"

3"

2"
2"

9"

9⁄₃₂" shank hole ¾" counterbore on bottom side

8"

3"

18"

¼" × 3" lag screws with ¼" flat washers

**EXPLODED VIEW**

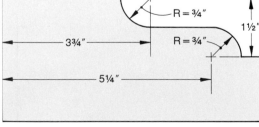

R = ¾"
R = ¾"
1½"
3¾"
5¼"

**STRETCHER ENDS**

SIDE RAIL TOP
(FULL-SIZED PATTERN)

# COLONIAL CANDLE BOX

**B**ecause they provided the only source of light other than the fireplace in colonial American homes, candles were important to our forefathers. Early American woodworkers built candle boxes to store and to protect this valuable commodity from heat and from mice, which feasted on the tallow shafts. Like many of the originals, the lid on our pine box contains a simple-to carve decorative design and thumb grasp. Larger versions of this same box were constructed to store family papers, records, and other valuable documents.

## First, machine the box parts

**1.** From ½" pine stock, cut a piece 3½" wide by 24" long for the box sides (A) and back (B). Now, cut the front (C) to the size listed in the Bill of Materials.

**2.** Cut a ¼" groove ¼" deep and ¼" from the top and bottom edges of the 24"-long piece. See the Exploded View drawing for reference. Now, cut the same-sized groove ¼" from the bottom edge of the front piece. (We used a ¼" dado blade to make the cuts. You also could fit your table-mounted router with a ¼" straight bit and fence to form the groove.)

**3.** Crosscut the sides (A) and back (B) to length from the 24"-long grooved board.

**4.** Cut the box bottom (D) to size from ¼" plywood. (We cut the bottom $\frac{1}{16}$" smaller in length and width than the opening to allow for expansion and contraction of the box.) Dry-clamp the box together to check the fit.

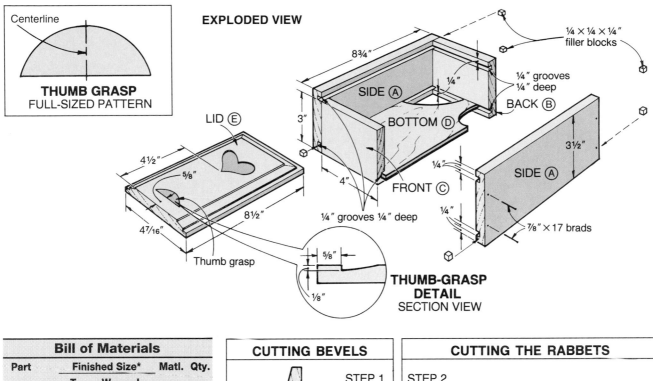

**THUMB GRASP**
FULL-SIZED PATTERN

Centerline

**EXPLODED VIEW**

8¾″

SIDE Ⓐ

BOTTOM Ⓓ

BACK Ⓑ

¼ × ¼ × ¼″
filler blocks

¼″ grooves
¼″ deep

3″

4″

FRONT Ⓒ

¼″

¼″ grooves ¼″ deep

SIDE Ⓐ

3½″

⅞″ × 17 brads

¼″

LID Ⓔ

4½″

5⁄8″

8½″

4⁷⁄₁₆″

Thumb grasp

5⁄8″

1⁄8″

**THUMB-GRASP DETAIL**
SECTION VIEW

## Bill of Materials

| Part | Finished Size* | | | Matl. | Qty. |
|---|---|---|---|---|---|
| | T | W | L | | |
| A* sides | ½″ | 3½″ | 8¾″ | P | 2 |
| B* back | ½″ | 3½″ | 4″ | P | 1 |
| C front | ½″ | 3″ | 4″ | P | 1 |
| D bottom | ¼″ | 4⁷⁄₁₆″ | 8³⁄₁₆″ | PW | 1 |
| E lid | ½″ | 4⁷⁄₁₆″ | 8½″ | P | 1 |

*Initially cut parts marked with an * oversized. Trim each to the finished size listed according to the how-to instructions.

**Material Key:** P-pine, PW-plywood
**Supplies:** double-faced tape, ⅞″x 17 brads, finish.

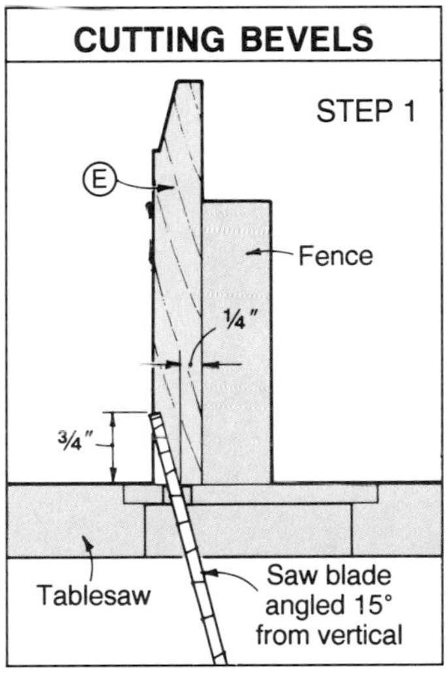

### CUTTING BEVELS

STEP 1

Ⓔ

Fence

¼″

¾″

Tablesaw

Saw blade angled 15° from vertical

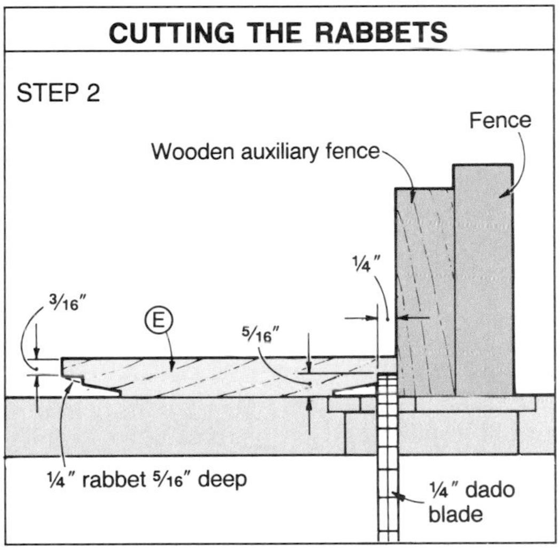

### CUTTING THE RABBETS

STEP 2

Wooden auxiliary fence

Fence

¼″

3⁄16″

Ⓔ

5⁄16″

¼″ rabbet 5⁄16″ deep

¼″ dado blade

## Assemble box and plug the grooves

**1.** Glue and clamp the box (do not glue the bottom in place; you want it to float in the grooves).

**2.** Nail the box together with ⅞″x17 brads. Check for square. Using a nail set, indent the nails slightly below the pine surface.

**3.** Cut a piece of pine to ¼ x¼″ by 12″ long (we used a dovetail saw). Crosscut six pieces ⅜″ long from the strip for the groove filler blocks. See the Exploded View drawing for reference.

**4.** Glue the filler blocks in the ends of the exposed grooves. Let the glue dry, and then trim and

sand the ends of the blocks flush with the surfaces of the box.

## Cut and shape the lid; then sand and add the finish

**1.** Cut the lid (E) to size. Using carbon paper, transfer the full-sized heart pattern to the top of the lid where located on the Exploded View drawing.

**2.** Carve the outline of the heart with a hobby knife (we cut about ⅛″ deep). Using a ¼″ chisel (you could also use a carving gouge if you have one), remove the stock inside the cut outline as shown in

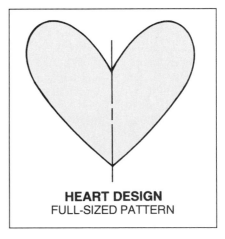

**HEART DESIGN**
FULL-SIZED PATTERN

*continued*

# COLONIAL CANDLE BOX
*continued*

the photo *below.* (We used double-faced tape to hold the lid securely to our workbench top when we carved the heart.) For a more realistic look, leave the faceted chisel cuts visible.

**After outlining the heart with a hobby knife, remove the stock with a chisel.**

**3.** Transfer the thumb grasp outline to the lid. Then, shape the thumb grasp using the procedure listed in step one and the Thumb Grasp detail accompanying the Exploded View drawing.

**4.** Using Step 1 of the drawing on page 59 for reference, cut a bevel along three sides of the lid. Switch to a ¼" dado blade and refer to Step 2 above to cut the rabbet along the same three lid sides. Check the fit of the lid in the grooves in the box; trim if necessary for smooth operation.

**5.** Sand the box and lid.

### Add the painted antique finish

**1.** Distress the unpainted surface. Antiques usually have their fair share of dings, nicks, and scratches. But before you go about blemishing the surface of your new project, imagine where the object would have received the greatest wear through the years. Then, plan

your distressing accordingly. You can use a ball peen hammer to simulate dents, a screwdriver to make scratches, and a rasp to scuff heavily used areas. Then, gently round the edges and corners with 80-grit sandpaper wrapped around a 1" dowel as shown *below.* For a natural "worn" look, remember to sand the edges unevenly from spot to spot.

**For an edge-rounding tool, wrap 80-grit sandpaper around a 1" dowel.**

And, don't overdo it. If a surface would have received little wear over the years, leave it alone. As one expert told us: "You want to distress—not destroy."

**2.** Apply the finish in layers as shown in the photo *opposite.* This process yields great results, but it does require up to seven coats of finishes. So, be patient. As you'll see in Step 3, these multiple layers will lead to the aged look you're after.

To start, wipe on a dark stain and let dry. Then, apply two protective layers of a clear finish (preferably polyurethane), and lightly sand the second coat before laying down a primer paint. The

primer can be any paint, but it should be close in color to one of the favorite colonial primer colors: iron-oxide red (our favorite), black, or mustard yellow.

After the primer dries, follow up with the color coat.

Latex and oil-based paints work fine, and you can apply one over the other. However, always sand an oil-based paints work fine, and you can apply one over the other. However, always sand an oil-based paint before applying a latex finish over it. Otherwise, the latex material may pool or not adhere properly.

**3.** Now, roll back the years by using 320-grit sandpaper to wear away the color coat along edges, corners, and other areas where the paint would have worn off through use. Although 320-grit paper loads up fast, a coarser paper cuts too quickly through the various layers. First, lightly sand the entire surface, then sand down to the primer coat around hard-use areas as shown *below.* If you should accidentally sand through the primer, the two clear coats will protect the stained

**320-grit sandpaper helps you remove the color coat without sanding through the primer.**

**To simulate patina, leave accumulations of a dark gel stain in the nooks and crannies of the surface.**

**After practicing your spattering technique on paper, give the project a uniform coat of fine speckles.**

wood. Since old wood is darker than new wood, try not to reveal the bare wood.

**4.** Patina in five minutes? Sure! Just apply a coat of dark oil-based gel stain over the surface, then wipe away most of it with a lint-free cloth as shown *left*. Leave deposits in crevices and other areas not likely to have received wear and cleaning over the years. The residue left behind after you remove the stain simulates the buildup of grime referred to as "patina."

**5.** Add a bit more character by spattering the surface. To achieve this accent (called "fly specks" by some), first mix two parts gel stain with one part mineral spirits in a shallow container. Then, dab an old toothbrush, or a paintbrush with its bristles trimmed to ½" long, into the mixture. Practice your spattering technique on a piece of paper before trying it on your project. Place the brush about 6" from the paper, and run your finger through the bristles. When you feel you have the right touch, add a uniform spattering of fine speckles to the workpiece as we're doing below. Don't overdo it. A little spattering goes a long way.

***Note:*** *Spattering and antiquing work well on non-wood surfaces, too. For example, see page 66 where we aged a clock face.*

Now read the section on finishing the sofa table for the names of the paints and finishes we used.

**Project Tool Guide**
Tablesaw
 Dado blade or dado set

***Note:*** *We built this project using the tools listed. You may be able to substitute other tools and equipment for listed items you don't have. You'll also need various common hand tools and clamps to complete the project.*

# EARLY-AMERICAN CANDLESTAND

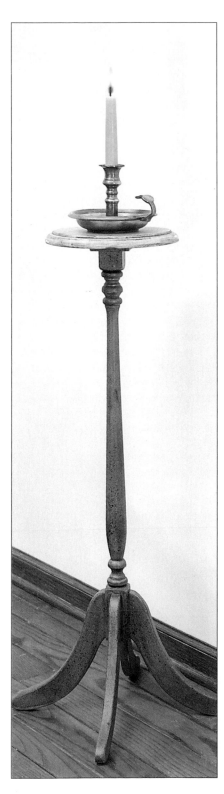

**N**owadays, most people use a candlestand as a decorative accent. But during the early years of this nation, it was an important piece of furniture for quite a different reason. If someone wanted to pursue a hobby such as reading or needlework, he or she needed sufficient light nearby. The candlestand, which was lightweight enough to move to the desired location, provided the perfect platform for that light source—the candle. Today, you can take a shortcut by substituting a 2x2x30" baluster for the turned pedestal. Turned balusters—used to support hand railings—are available at most homecenters.

*Note: Like the originals, our candlestand is designed for candles and small objects. If you wish to use the stand for larger items, increase the spread of the legs and the diameter of the top for more stability.*

**Start with the legs**

**1.** Using the Leg Pattern on page 64 for reference, use tracing paper or a photocopy machine to make a copy. (We made a photocopy, adhered it to ⅛" hardboard with spray-on adhesive, and then cut the

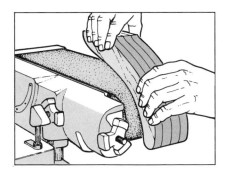

hardboard template to shape on a bandsaw.) Cut the paper pattern to shape, and use it as a template to mark four leg outlines on ¾"-thick pine stock.

**2.** Bandsaw the legs (A) to shape. Using double-faced tape, tape together the legs, face-to-face, with the edges and ends flush. Using the round end of a stationary or belt sander, sand the edges of the legs flush as shown *below left*.

**3.** Using a square, mark the dowel-hole locations on each leg. Separate the legs and remove the double-faced tape.

**4.** As shown on page 64, use a doweling jig and drill ⅜" holes ¾" deep where marked.

**5.** Rout or sand a ⅛" round-over on all edges of each leg, *except* those that will fit against the baluster. See the drawing *opposite* for reference. Sand the legs.

**A turned pedestal that requires no lathe**

**1.** If you're a turner, you might enjoy turning the pedestal. If not, buy a 2x2x30" baluster. (We used a Mansion Industries 2x2x30" traditional baluster, part no. P230TR.) Although it's called a 2x2 baluster, ours measured 1⅜" square. Crosscut the top end for a 28" finished length.

**2.** Mark reference centerlines on the bottom of the pedestal where shown on the drawing *opposite*. Mark a second line perpendicular to the first line and ¾" from the bottom of the pedestal.

**3.** Insert a pair of ⅜" dowel centers into the dowel holes in one leg. Align the dowel centers on the reference lines and squeeze the pieces together to transfer the hole centerpoints to the pedestal.

**4.** Drill ⅜" holes ⅞" deep into the pedestal where marked. Sand the pedestal smooth.

## Now, add the legs to the pedestal

**1.** Glue a pair of ⅜" dowel pins 1½" long in each leg.

**2.** Clamp a handscrew clamp to each leg where shown in the photo *below*. (We wrapped sandpaper between the leg and clamp to prevent the clamp from slipping.)

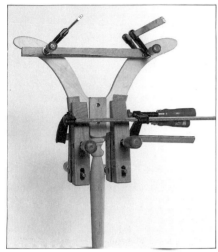

**Handscrew clamps provide the necessary flat surfaces for aligning the legs with sliding-head clamps.**

**3.** Using a pair of sliding-head clamps, clamp two legs to the pedestal by placing the clamp jaws on the handscrew clamps where shown *above*. To help keep the legs parallel, clamp a piece of scrap stock to the legs as shown at the top of the photo.

**4.** After the glue dries, remove the clamps and redrill the remaining four holes in the baluster to ⅞" deep. (The dowel pins installed with the first two legs reduce some of the depth.) Using the same procedure as in Steps 1 and 2, glue, dowel, and clamp the remaining two legs to the pedestal.

## And to top things off...

**1.** Edge-join two ¾" pieces of flat stock 5" wide by 10" long. (To prevent cupping later, don't use one solid piece for the top. Even if it's flat now, a piece this wide will tend to cup over time.)

*continued*

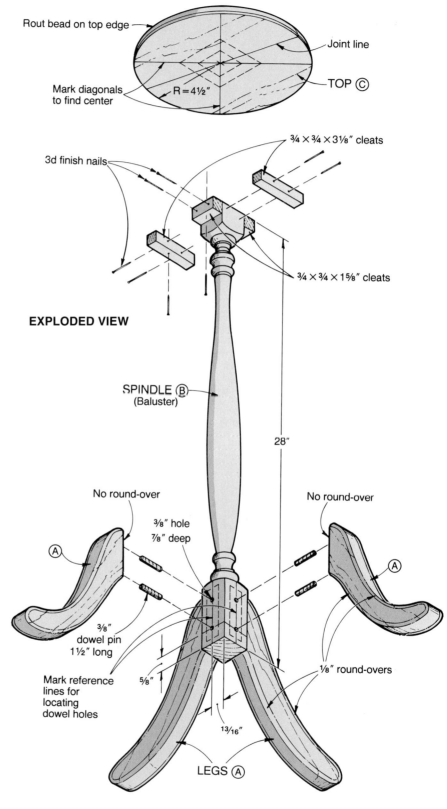

Rout bead on top edge

Joint line

Mark diagonals to find center

R = 4½"

TOP Ⓒ

¾ × ¾ × 3⅛" cleats

3d finish nails

¾ × ¾ × 1⅝" cleats

**EXPLODED VIEW**

SPINDLE Ⓑ
(Baluster)

28"

No round-over

No round-over

⅜" hole
⅞" deep

Ⓐ

Ⓐ

⅜"
dowel pin
1½" long

⅛" round-overs

Mark reference lines for locating dowel holes

⅝"

13/16"

LEGS Ⓐ

# EARLY-AMERICAN CANDLESTAND
*continued*

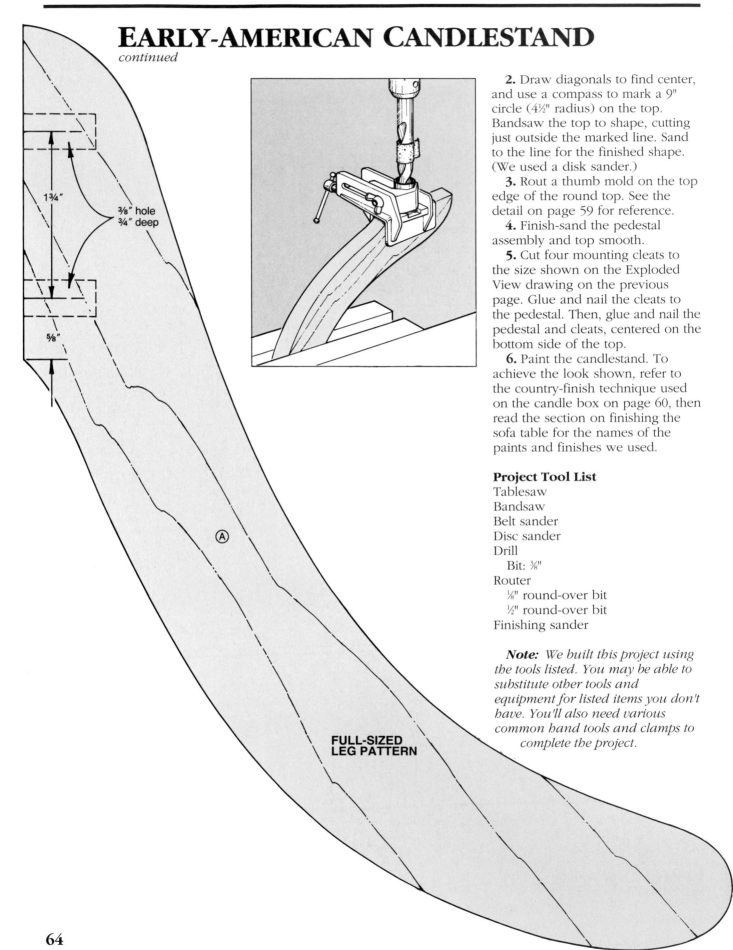

1¾"

⅜" hole
¾" deep

⅝"

Ⓐ

**FULL-SIZED
LEG PATTERN**

**2.** Draw diagonals to find center, and use a compass to mark a 9" circle (4½" radius) on the top. Bandsaw the top to shape, cutting just outside the marked line. Sand to the line for the finished shape. (We used a disk sander.)

**3.** Rout a thumb mold on the top edge of the round top. See the detail on page 59 for reference.

**4.** Finish-sand the pedestal assembly and top smooth.

**5.** Cut four mounting cleats to the size shown on the Exploded View drawing on the previous page. Glue and nail the cleats to the pedestal. Then, glue and nail the pedestal and cleats, centered on the bottom side of the top.

**6.** Paint the candlestand. To achieve the look shown, refer to the country-finish technique used on the candle box on page 60, then read the section on finishing the sofa table for the names of the paints and finishes we used.

**Project Tool List**
Tablesaw
Bandsaw
Belt sander
Disc sander
Drill
   Bit: ⅜"
Router
   ⅛" round-over bit
   ½" round-over bit
Finishing sander

*Note: We built this project using the tools listed. You may be able to substitute other tools and equipment for listed items you don't have. You'll also need various common hand tools and clamps to complete the project.*

# PILGRIM'S-PRIDE WALL BOX

**T**his simple project has its roots planted firmly in colonial America. But back then, boxes of this shape couldn't have held matches—they weren't invented until 1816. Rather, colonists stored delicate, long-stemmed clay pipes in similar wall-hung boxes.

### Cut the parts and carve the heart

**1.** From ¼" pine (we resawed ¾" stock to this thickness), cut a piece 2¼" wide by 13¾" long for the box back (A). Use carbon paper to transfer the full-sized top pattern outline and hole centerpoint to one end of the pine. Drill the ¼" hole, and cut the back to shape.

**2.** Cut the sides (B), front (C), and bottom (D) to the sizes shown at *right*.

**3.** Transfer the full-sized heart pattern shown on page 59 to the front piece (C).

**4.** Carve the outline of the heart with an X-acto (we cut about ⅛" deep). Using a ¼" chisel, remove the stock inside the cut outline. (We used double-faced tape to hold the back securely to our workbench top when we carved the heart.)

**5.** Apply glue to the mating surfaces, and hold the box together with tape. Nail together the box with ½"×18 brads. Using a nail set, indent the nails slightly below the wood's surface.

**6.** Sand and paint the box. To achieve the country look as shown, refer to the country-finish technique in the Candle Box project on page 60. Then, read the section on finishing the sofa table for the names of the paints and finishes we used.

**Supplies:** double-faced tape, ½"×18 brads, finish.

### Project Tool List
Tablesaw
Bandsaw or scrollsaw
Drill
  Bit: ¼"
Finishing sander

**Note:** *We built this project using the tools listed. You may be able to substitute other tools and equipment for listed items you don't have. You'll also need various common hand tools and clamps to complete the project.*

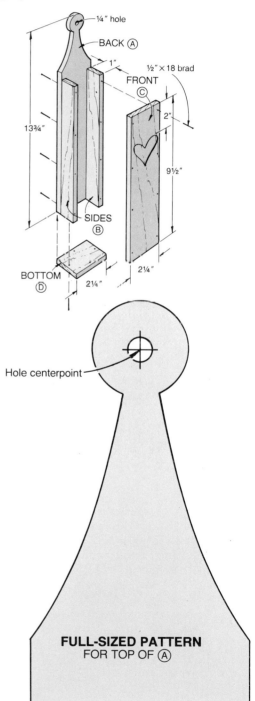

Hole centerpoint

**FULL-SIZED PATTERN**
FOR TOP OF Ⓐ

# COUNTRY CLOCK

**C**locks were a luxury item in America during the early years. Only the wealthy could afford to have one imported from England. In fact, it wasn't until around 1800, and the invention of the relatively inexpensive mantel or shelf clock, that timepieces came to

the masses. Boy, how times have changed!

We ran across the idea for this wall clock (vintage unknown) in a small antique store in Massachusetts. It's powered by an easy-to-install quartz movement.

**Start with the clock front**

**1.** Cut two pieces of ¾"-thick pine stock to 6½" wide by 13½" long. Glue and clamp the pieces edge to edge for the clock front (A). Immediately remove excess glue with a damp cloth or by scraping lightly with a scraper.

**2.** After the glue dries, remove the clamps, and trim the clock front (A) to 12½" square.

**3.** Draw diagonals on the clock front to find center. With a compass, mark a 4½" radius (9"-diameter) on the clock front. Drill a blade start hole on the inside of the marked circle, and use a jigsaw or scrollsaw to cut just on the inside of the marked circle. Then, drum-sand to the line. (As shown in the photo at *right,* we taped spacers to the bottom of the clock front to raise it above the surface of the drill-press table.)

**4.** Rout a ½" round-over along the front edge of the opening where shown on the Exploded View drawing. Switch bits, and rout a ¼" rabbet ¼" deep along the back edge of the opening.

**5.** Next, rout a ¼" round-over along the outside edges of the clock front. Keep this bit in your router; you'll use it to rout the frame members. Sand the clock front smooth.

### The frame comes next

**1.** Cut two pieces of ¾"-thick pine to 2" wide by 30" long.

**2.** Rout ¼" round-overs along one edge of each piece.

**Support the clock front on spacers to drum-sand the opening.**

**3.** Miter-cut the frame pieces (B) to 14" long. Glue and nail the frame pieces to the clock front (A). Be sure the frame members are flush with the clock front, and sand.

### You're almost done

**1.** Trace the clock-face outline and shaft opening onto a piece of ¼" hardboard or plywood for the dial backing (D). (See the Buying Guide for our source of the dial and movement.)

**2.** Drill a ⅜" shaft hole through the backing, and then cut and sand the backing to shape.

**3.** Adhere the dial to the backing. (We used double-faced tape; epoxy also would work.) Check the fit of the dial and backing into the rabbet in the clock front. (We had to belt-sand the edges of our dial and backing to make it fit.)

**4.** To "age" the dial, lightly handsand the front of the dial with 320-grit sandpaper on a wooden block. Then, dampen a cloth with a bit of stain and lightly wipe the front of the dial.

**5.** Finish as desired. To duplicate the finish we used, refer to the country-finish technique in the Candle Box project on page 60. Then, turn to the section on finishing the sofa table for the paints and finishes we used.

**6.** Secure the dial and backing in the rabbet with hotmelt adhesive. Mount the clock movement to the dial and backing. Snip ¼" off the end of the minute hand. Finally, add the hands and hang.

### Buying Guide

• **Dial and movement.** 9½"-diameter schoolhouse dial and a high-torque quartz movement with black hands. Kit no. 71044. For current price, contact Klockit, PO Box 636, Lake Geneva, WI 53147, or call 800-556-2548 to order.

### Project Tool List

Tablesaw
Scrollsaw
Drill press
  Bit: ⅜"
Drum sander
Router
  ¼" rabbeting bit
  ¼" round-over bit
  ½" round-over bit
Finishing sander

*Note: We built this project using the tools listed. You may be able to substitute other tools and equipment for listed items you don't have. You'll also need various common hand tools and clamps to complete the project.*

**EXPLODED VIEW**

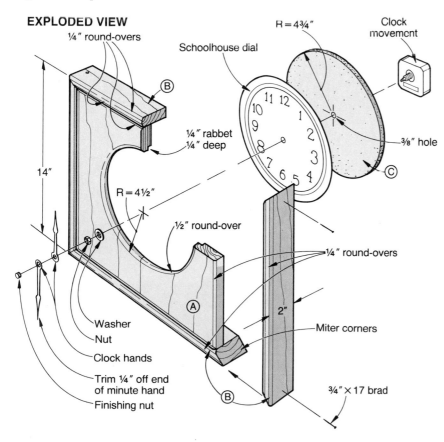

¼" round-overs

B

Schoolhouse dial

R = 4¾"

Clock movement

14"

¼" rabbet
¼" deep

R = 4½"

½" round-over

¾" hole

C

¼" round-overs

A

2"

Miter corners

Washer

Nut

Clock hands

Trim ¼" off end of minute hand

Finishing nut

B

¾" × 17 brad

# COUNTRY FURNITURE

*A trestle table, Shaker chairs, buffet, sofa table, and bench—
the following furniture projects are designed for living in the
country tradition.*

# TRESTLE TABLE

**Trestle tables date back hundreds of years, and were common in the Middle Ages. The early tables consisted of loose boards temporarily set on trestles—open, braced frames. The table has undergone many changes in design to meet the needs of those who built it. The Shakers, for instance, designed and constructed many variations—some up to 20' long—for communal dining.**

### Start with the uprights

**1.** Rip and crosscut eight pieces of ¾"-thick oak to 2⅞" wide by 24½" long for the four uprights (A).

**2.** With the best surfaces facing out, glue and clamp two pieces together for each upright. Check that the ends and edges are flush. Later, scrape off the excess glue, and plane or joint 1⁄16" off each edge to ensure flatness. Trim both ends of each upright for a 23½" length.

### Add the feet and table supports

**1.** Cut eight pieces of ¾" oak to 3⅛" wide by 29" long for the two feet (B). For each foot, laminate four pieces together face to face, keeping the ends and edges flush and the best sides facing out.

**2.** Scrape the excess glue off the edges (not the ends) of each foot. Plane or joint 1⁄16" off each edge for a 3" finished width.

**3.** Using the Foot Grid drawing on page 70, make a paper template for the side profile. To do this, start by cutting a piece of paper to 3X14",

*continued*

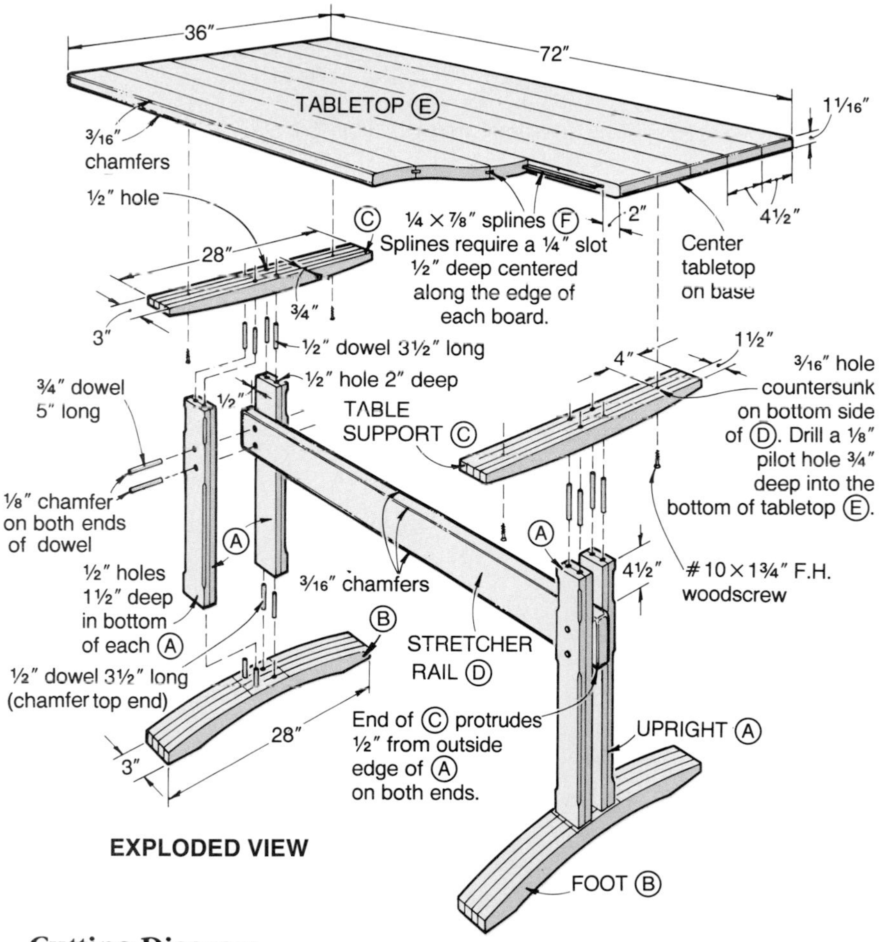

36"
72"
TABLETOP (E)
3⁄16" chamfers
1⁄16"
½" hole
(C)
¼ × ⅞" splines (F)
Splines require a ¼" slot ½" deep centered along the edge of each board.
2"
4½"
Center tabletop on base
28"
3"
¾"
½" dowel 3½" long
½" hole 2" deep
TABLE SUPPORT (C)
4"
1½"
3⁄16" hole countersunk on bottom side of (D). Drill a ⅛" pilot hole ¾" deep into the bottom of tabletop (E).
¾" dowel 5" long
⅛" chamfer on both ends of dowel
(A)
½" holes 1½" deep in bottom of each (A)
3⁄16" chamfers
4½"
#10 × 1¾" F.H. woodscrew
(B)
STRETCHER RAIL (D)
½" dowel 3½" long (chamfer top end)
28"
3"
End of (C) protrudes ½" from outside edge of (A) on both ends.
UPRIGHT (A)
FOOT (B)
EXPLODED VIEW


| Bill of Materials | | | | | |
|---|---|---|---|---|---|
| **Part** | **Finished Size*** | | | **Mat.** | **Qty.** |
| | **T** | **W** | **L** | | |
| A* | 1½" | 2¾" | 23½" | oak (lami.) | 4 |
| B* | 3" | 3" | 28" | oak (lam.) | 2 |
| C* | 3" | 1½" | 28" | oak (lami.) | 2 |
| D* | 1½" | 5" | 57" | oak (lam.) | 1 |
| E* | 1⅟16" | 36" | 72" | oak (laml.) | 1 |
| F | ¼" | ⅞" | 67½" | hardboard | 7 |

*Parts marked with an * are cut larger initially, and then trimmed to finished size. Please read the how-to instructions before cutting.

**Supplies:** ½" dowel stock, ¾" oak dowel stock, #10 x 1¾" flathead wood screws, stain, polyurethane sanding sealer, polyurethane, 0000 steel wool, paste furniture wax.

### Cutting Diagram

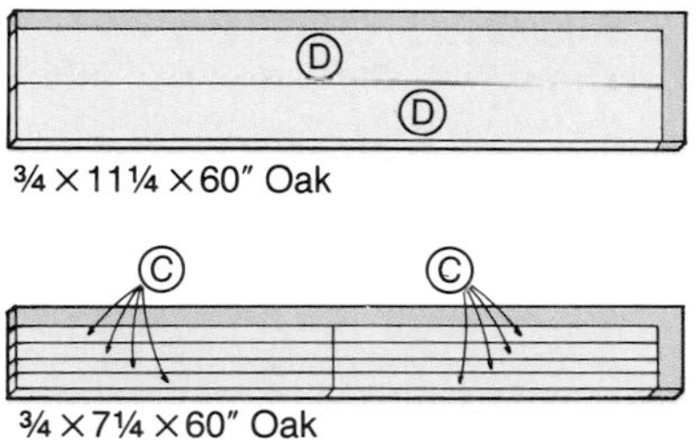

(D)
(D)
¾ × 11¼ × 60" Oak
(C)
(C)
¾ × 7¼ × 60" Oak


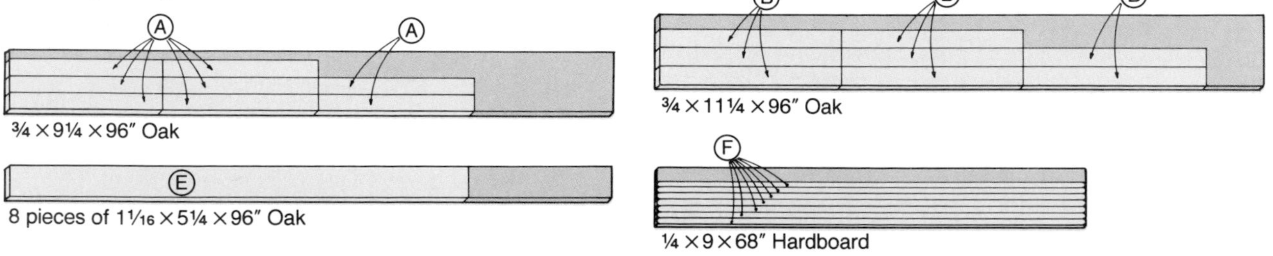

(A)
(A)
¾ × 9¼ × 96" Oak
(E)
8 pieces of 1⅟16 × 5¼ × 96" Oak
(B)
(B)
(B)
¾ × 11¼ × 96" Oak
(F)
¼ × 9 × 68" Hardboard

# TRESTLE TABLE
*continued*

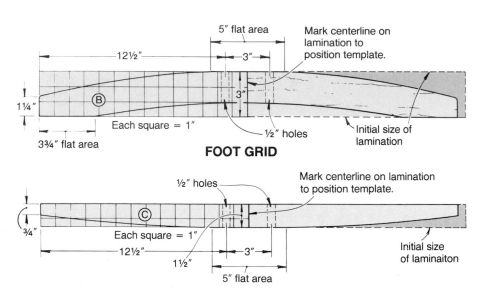

**FOOT GRID**

12½"  5" flat area  3"  Mark centerline on lamination to position template.

1¼"  Each square = 1"  3"

3¾" flat area  ½" holes  Initial size of lamination

½" holes  Mark centerline on lamination to position template.

¾"  Each square = 1"

12½"  1½"  3"  Initial size of laminaiton

5" flat area

**TABLE SUPPORT GRID**

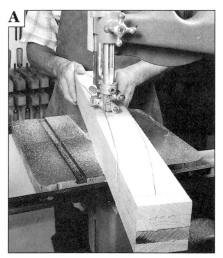

**Trace the template outline onto the foot lamination, and then cut the foot to shape on the bandsaw. Later, trim the ends square on a radial arm saw.**

and draw a 1" grid on the paper. Now, lay out the shape of half of one foot on the marked grid. Mark the points where the foot-pattern outline crosses each grid line. Then, draw lines to connect the points. Cut the paper template to shape.

**4.** Find and mark a centerline across each foot lamination (see the Foot Grid drawing for reference).

Position the inside edge of the paper template against the marked centerline, with the bottom edge of the template flush with the flat, bottom edge of the lamination. Carefully trace the foot outline onto each foot lamination. (You'll need to trace the half template twice to mark each complete foot.)

**5.** As shown in photo A at *left*, cut each foot to shape on a bandsaw fitted with a ¼" or larger blade. To ensure a level-sitting table, do not cut the three flat areas of the foot (see the Foot Grid drawing for reference). Finally, use a radialsaw or tablesaw and crosscut both ends of each foot square for a 28" finished length.

**6.** To make the table supports (C), cut eight pieces of ¾" oak to 1⅝" wide by 29" long. Glue and clamp four pieces together face to face for each support. Later, scrape off the excess glue and plane 1⁄16" off each edge for a 1½"-finished width.

**7.** Using the procedure described in Steps 3, 4, and 5 *above,* make a 2x14" paper template, cut the template to shape, and align with the top, flat edge of the lamination. Trace its outline onto each lamination. Now, cut the supports to shape on the bandsaw.

**8.** Sand the edges on all the pieces smooth to remove saw marks.

### And now, for the stretcher rail

**1.** Cut two pieces of ¾"-thick oak to 5⅛" wide by 58" long for the stretcher rail (D). Glue and clamp the pieces together face to face with the edges and ends flush.

**2.** Later, remove the clamps and scrape off the excess glue. Plane 1⁄16" off both edges to ensure flatness, and then trim the ends for a 57" finished length.

**3.** Rout 3⁄16" chamfers along all edges and ends of the stretcher rail.

### Next, laminate the tabletop

**1.** Rip and crosscut eight pieces of 1 1⁄16"- thick oak (five-quarter stock) to 4⅝" wide by 73" long for the tabletop (E). Plane 1⁄16" off each edge to remove the saw marks and to ensure even joints when laminating.

**2.** Position the pieces, best side up, on a work surface. Arrange the pieces for the best grain pattern, and number them one through eight for ease of assembly later.

**3.** Chuck a ¼" slot-cutting bit into your router. Rout a ¼" slot ½" deep, centered from top to bottom, along mating edges of the tabletop pieces. Stop the slots 2½" from each end.

**4.** Cut seven splines (F) to size from ¼" hardboard. Sand the spline ends to a tapered shape. With the splines in place, dry-clamp the first four pieces of the tabletop together to check for tight-fitting joints. Repeat with the other four pieces for the other tabletop half.

**5.** Glue, spline, and clamp the first four pieces together, keeping the edges, ends, and surfaces flat. Repeat with the second four pieces. Later, glue, spline, and clamp the two tabletop halves together as shown in photo B *opposite*.

**6.** Remove the clamps and scrape off the excess glue. Crosscut each end for a finished length of 72". (To minimize chipping the good face of the tabletop, we placed it upside down on saw horses. Then we clamped a straightedge square with the sides, and trimmed ½" off each end with a portable circular saw

**B**

Glue, spline, and clamp the two tabletop halves together, clamping long scrap pieces to the top and bottom to ensure flatness.

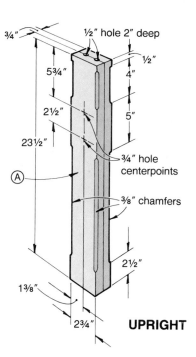

½" hole 2" deep

¾"

5¾"

½"

4"

2½"

5"

23½"

A

¾" hole centerpoints

⅜" chamfers

2½"

1⅜"

2¾"

**UPRIGHT**

fitted with a carbide-tipped blade.) Belt-sand the tabletop.

### Rout the chamfers

**1.** Using the Upright drawing as a guide, mark chamfer start-and-stop lines across each upright (A). Then, rout ⅜" chamfers *between* the marked lines. (When routing the chamfers, we wore a full-face shield. The shield allowed us to keep a close look at the rotating bit for starting and stopping at the marked lines.)

**2.** Now, rout a ³⁄₁₆" chamfer on top and bottom edges of the tabletop.

**3.** Using a palm or finish sander, finish-sand the tabletop and uprights. Then, finish-sand the remaining pieces.

### Assemble the base

**1.** To attach the uprights to the stretcher, start by building a pair of supports to the size shown in the drawing *above right*. (We found the jigs extremely helpful in holding the stretcher rail in position when clamping it between the uprights.)

**2.** Measure in ½" from each end of the stretcher rail, and mark a line across both sides of each end (four lines in all). The lines will help you align the rail with the uprights in the next step.

**3.** Apply glue to the mating surfaces, and position the stretcher rail on the two support jigs and

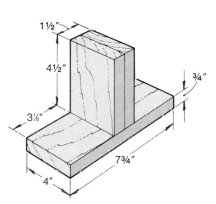

1½"

4½"

3⅛"

¾"

7¾"

4"

between the two uprights as shown in photo C on page 72. With the stretcher rail protruding ½" beyond the outside edge of the uprights (use the lines drawn in the previous step for this), clamp the stretcher rail in place. Check that the stretcher is square with the uprights as shown in photo C. Also make sure that the uprights are square with each other as shown in photo D. Immediately wipe off any excess glue with a damp cloth. Let the glue dry, and then repeat the procedure on the opposite end with the two remaining uprights.

**4.** Locate and mark the center-points of the two ¾" holes on each upright (see the Upright drawing for location). As shown in photo E, clamp the stretcher rail-upright assembly to your workbench, and clamp a scrap block onto the bottom face of the lower upright where shown in the photo. (The

scrap block helps prevent chip-out when boring through the bottom upright.) Bore a pair of ¾" holes where marked through the uprights and stretcher. Repeat this procedure for the other end.

**5.** Cut four 5" lengths of ¾" oak dowel. Chamfer each end of each dowel (we used a belt sander). Apply glue in the ¾" holes in the stretcher-upright joint, and drive the dowels in place with a rubber mallet so ¼" of dowel protrudes from each surface. Immediately wipe off any excess glue.

**6.** As shown in photo F, position the base upside down and resting on the supports. Position the flat, center portion of a foot on the ends of the uprights and clamp the assembly to your workbench.

**7.** Use a square to transfer each upright joint line (the glue line between the two individual pieces that form each upright) up the outside face and across the bottom of the foot. (The line is just to the right of the clamp in photo F.) Next, transfer the second line across the bottom of the foot. Mark centerpoints at the first and third glue line on the bottom of the foot. Bore four ½" holes through the foot and 1½" deep into the upright. Repeat the marking and boring procedure with the other foot. *continued*

# TRESTLE TABLE
*continued*

Position and clamp the uprights and stretcher on a support jig. With a framing square, check that both uprights are square with the stretcher.

Use a small square to check that the uprights are square and parallel.

Mark the centerpoints and bore a pair of ¾" holes through the upright stretcher rail assembly, backing the stock to prevent chip-out.

Clamp the foot to the uprights. Mark the centerpoints, and bore the holes for the dowels.

**8.** Cut eight pieces of ½" dowel to 3½" long. Sand a chamfer on one end of each dowel.

**9.** One at a time, clamp a dowel in a bench vise, and cut a ⅛"-deep glue groove (kerf) the length of the dowel. (We used a dovetail saw to cut each kerf.)

**10.** Spread glue in the dowel holes, and glue and drive the dowels through the bottom of the feet and into the uprights. Drive the dowels until the bottom of the dowels are flush with the bottom surface of the feet. Trim or sand any protruding dowels flush if necessary. Repeat for the other foot on the opposite end.

**11.** Use the process just described in Steps 5, 6, and 7 to join the oak table supports to the top ends of the uprights.

## Apply the finish

**1.** Apply the stain of your choice. Apply two coats of polyurethane sanding sealer to all surfaces (including the bottom of the tabletop), sanding with 320-grit paper between coats.

**2.** Apply two coats of clear poly-urethane. (We used satin poly-urethane. After the final coat dried, we applied paste furniture wax to 0000 steel wool, and rubbed the surface down for a smooth finish.)

## Assemble the table

**1.** Lay the tabletop facedown on a blanket. Center the base, also upside down, on the bottom of the tabletop. Being careful not to drill too deep, drill a ³⁄₁₆" shank hole through the table support, and a ⅛" pilot hole ¾" deep into the bottom side of the tabletop, where located on the Exploded View drawing. Fasten the base to the tabletop with #10x1¾" wood screws.

## Project Tool List
Tablesaw
Bandsaw
Jointer
Router
  ¼" slot-cutting bit
  Chamfering bit
Drill press
  Bits: ⅛", ³⁄₁₆", ½", ¾"
Belt sander
Finishing sander

***Note:*** *We built this project using the tools listed. You may be able to substitute other tools and equipment for listed items you don't have. You'll also need various common hand tools and clamps to complete the project.*

# SHAKER SIMPLICITY CHAIRS

**O**f all the magnificent designs Shaker furnituremakers left behind as a testament to their skills, none is more universally recognized than the ladder-back chair. Not only was this the most widely sold chair they made, it's also one of their most handsome.

Our chair derives its enduring utilitarian lines from a Harvard Shaker chair built around 1850. Adhere closely to measured drawings, but raised the seat about 1" for comfort, and eliminated finials from the chair back for simplicity.

After you construct our jig and drilling guide, you can build a set of chairs with ease.

### Start with the chair-leg jig: It's a real time saver

*Note: The key to drilling and routing the holes and mortises in the correct location in each chair leg is accomplished with our chair-leg jig and drill guide. Take your time when building the jig and guide.*

**1.** From ¾" plywood, cut the chair-leg jig parts (A, B, C, D) to the sizes listed in the Bill of Materials. [We resawed a piece of ¾"-thick plywood to form the ½"-thick layer (C). You could use ½" plywood.]

**2.** With the inside edges and ends flush, glue and nail together the bottom three layers (A, B, C) where shown on the End View drawing. Keep the gap between parts B and C exactly 1¼" the entire length of the jig for a snug fit of the 1¼"-diameter leg dowels.

**3.** For this jig to work as it should, you must position the top two layers of the jig (D) so that the router will be centered over the 1¼" recess (and ultimately over the chair-leg dowels). *continued*

# SHAKER SIMPLICITY CHAIRS
*continued*

Refer to the End View drawing for positioning particulars. Now, glue and nail the top layers into position.

**4.** Lay out and number the reference lines on the jig where shown on the Chair Leg Jig drawing.

**5.** Cut the dowel clamp (E) to size from ¾" solid stock (we used maple). Now, using carbon paper or by adhering a photocopy, transfer the centerlines for the 1¼" hole and the two ⁵⁄₃₂" holes, as well as reference marks A, B, C, from

the Dowel Clamp Drawing to the solid stock. Drill the 1¼" hole, and cut a ⅛"-wide slot to the 1¼" hole. Drill and countersink the two ⁵⁄₃₂" holes.

**6.** Center the hole in the dowel clamp against the 1¼"-wide recess, and screw the clamp to the end of the jig (see the End View for reference). Set the jig aside for now.

| Part | Finished Size | | | Mat. | Qty. |
|---|---|---|---|---|---|
| | T | W | L | | |
| **JIG AND DRILL GUIDE** | | | | | |
| A btm layer | ¾" | 9" | 46" | P | 1 |
| B 2nd layer | ¾" | 3⅞" | 46". | P | 2 |
| C 3rd layer | ½" | 3⅞" | 46". | P | 2 |
| D top layers | ¾" | 1½" | 46" | P | 4 |
| E dow clamp | ¾" | 1½" | 2¼" | M | 1 |
| F drill guide | ¾" | * | 11" | P | 2 |

**Bill of Materials**

**Material Key:** P-plywood, M-maple

*This dimension will depend on the diameter of your router base. See End View and Drill Guide drawings and read the instructions for determining this dimension.

**Supplies:** 6d finish nails, #8 x 1½" flathead wood screws, finish.

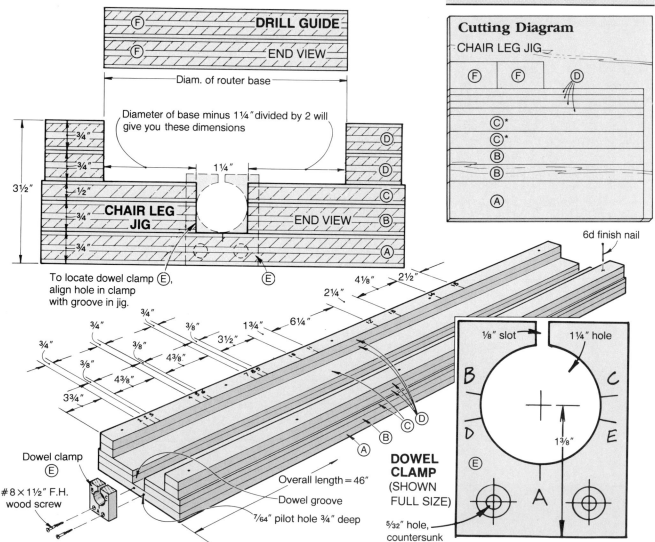

## DRILL GUIDE TOP VIEW

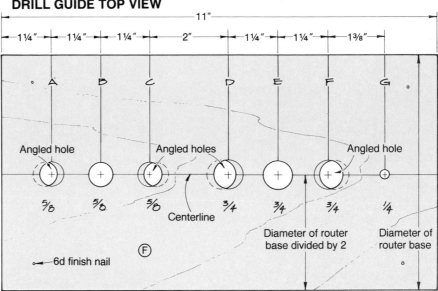

11"

1¼" 1¼" 1¼" 2" 1¼" 1¼" 1⅜"

A B C D E F G

Angled hole  Angled holes  Angled hole

⅝ ⅝ ⅝ ¾ ¾ ¾ ¼

Centerline

Diameter of router base divided by 2

Diameter of router base

(F)

6d finish nail

## DRILL GUIDE SECTION VIEW

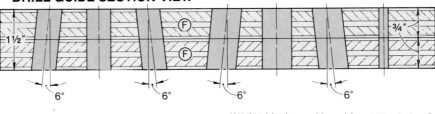

1½"   (F)   (F)   ¾"

6° 6° 6° 6°

Wedge blocks positioned for drilling holes C and F. (Place 1⅛"-high end under opposite end of guide to drill holes A and D.)

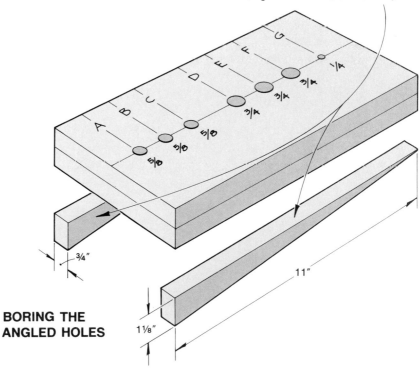

A B C D E F G

⅝ ⅝ ⅝ ¾ ¾ ¼

¾"

11"

1⅛"

**BORING THE ANGLED HOLES**

## Build the drill guide

**1.** From ¾" plywood, cut the two guide pieces (F) 11" long and as wide as the diameter of your router base. Glue and nail the pieces together with the edges and ends flush. Later, scrape off the excess glue and check the fit of the guide in the chair-leg jig.

**2.** Mark a centerline along the length of the drill guide where shown on the Drill Guide Top View. Mark reference lines perpendicular to the centerline to locate centerpoints for the ¼", ⅝", and ¾" holes where shown on the drawing. Mark the letters and hole sizes on their corresponding reference lines where shown *right*.

**3.** Using brad-point drill bits and your drill press, bore the nonangled holes (B, E, G) through the guide.

**4.** To bore the angled holes, first cut a pair of wedge-shaped blocks to the size shown on the drawing *right*. Position the blocks under the drill guide on your drill-press table. With the wide end of the blocks nearest the end with hole A, drill the angled holes C and F. Rotate the blocks so the widest end is nearest the G hole, and drill the angled holes A and D.

*continued*

75

# SHAKER SIMPLICITY CHAIRS

*continued*

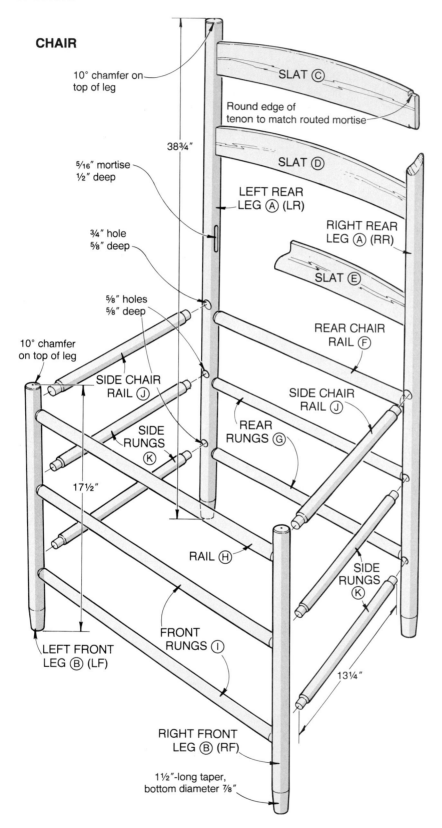

**CHAIR**

10° chamfer on top of leg

SLAT Ⓒ

Round edge of tenon to match routed mortise

38¾″

5/16″ mortise ½″ deep

SLAT Ⓓ

LEFT REAR LEG Ⓐ (LR)

¾″ hole 5/8″ deep

RIGHT REAR LEG Ⓐ (RR)

SLAT Ⓔ

5/8″ holes 5/8″ deep

REAR CHAIR RAIL Ⓕ

10° chamfer on top of leg

SIDE CHAIR RAIL Ⓙ

SIDE CHAIR RAIL Ⓙ

SIDE RUNGS Ⓚ

REAR RUNGS Ⓖ

17½″

SIDE RUNGS Ⓚ

RAIL Ⓗ

LEFT FRONT LEG Ⓑ (LF)

FRONT RUNGS Ⓘ

RIGHT FRONT LEG Ⓑ (RF)

1½″-long taper, bottom diameter 7/8″

13¼″

## Now, let's start building the chair

*Note:* *The instructions, Bill of Materials, Buying Guide, and Cutting Diagram give the directions and number of pieces needed to build a single chair. To make additional chairs, be sure to machine all identical pieces at the same time to ensure uniformity.*

**1.** Select the two straightest 48″-long dowels for the back legs (A). (We've noticed that nearly all of them have a slight bow—see the Buying Guide for our source.) To make sure both back legs bend in the same direction on the finished chair—toward the back—lay the dowels on a flat surface and position the bows as shown on the drawing *below*. Mark a reference line on one end of each dowel at the 6 o'clock position where shown on the drawing.

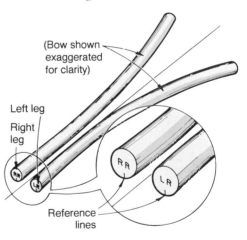

(Bow shown exaggerated for clarity)

Left leg

Right leg

RR

LR

RR

LR

Reference lines

**2.** Mark RR (for right rear) on the same end as the reference line on one oak dowel, and LR (for left rear) on the second dowel.

**3.** Slide the RR dowel into the 1¼″ recess in the jig and into the dowel clamp until the marked end of the dowel is flush with the outside face of the dowel clamp. Rotate the dowel to align the reference line on the dowel with reference line A on the dowel clamp as shown in the photo at *right*. The top edge of the dowel should be flush with the top face of jig parts C. You might have to tap the dowel in place with a rubber mallet.

**4.** Using a handscrew clamp, tighten the dowel clamp to prevent the dowel from turning in the jig when drilling the holes in the next step.

**5.** Position the drill guide in the jig, aligning reference line B on the drill guide with the marked number 1 on the jig as shown in the photo at *right*. Clamp the guide to the jig. Using a ⅝" brad-point bit, bore ⅝" deep into the dowel.

*Note: To prevent enlarging or changing the angle of the holes in the drill guide, lower the bit through the hole until it makes contact with the dowel. Start the drill and bore the hole. Stop the drill before removing it from the guide. (To drill the right depth, we wrapped tape on our bits.)*

**6.** Referring to the Drilling Guide Chart, move the drill guide to the second setting (B4), and drill a second ⅝" hole. Continue moving the guide along the jig and drill holes E7, G10, G11, G12, G13, G14, and G15 to the sizes noted on the chart.

**7.** To create the ½"-deep mortises for the chair-back slats, chuck a ⁵⁄₁₆" straight bit into your router. As shown in the photo at *right*, slowly lower the rotating bit into one ¼" hole and rout to the next ¼" hole. Be sure to grasp the router firmly—it tends to jerk entering the second ¼" hole when finishing the cut. Repeat this routing procedure to form the other mortises.

**8.** Remove the handscrew clamp from the dowel clamp. Twist the chair-leg dowel until the marked reference line on the end of the dowel aligns with reference line C on the dowel clamp. Again, secure the dowel in the dowel clamp. Drill holes C2, C5, and F8 as noted on the chart for the RR dowel.

**9.** Remove the RR leg from the jig and cut the top end for a finished length of 38¾". Using the Drilling Guide Chart, *continued*

**Align the ⅝" hole (reference line B) in the drill guide with the marked number 1 on the chair-leg jig, and drill a ⅝"-deep hole.**

**Lower the ⁵⁄₁₆" straight bit into the ¼" hole, and rout between a pair of ¼" holes to form the ⁵⁄₁₆" wide mortises for the backrest slats.**

77

# SHAKER SIMPLICITY CHAIRS
*continued*

| Drilling Guide Chart | | |
|---|---|---|
| Dowel-Clamp Setting | Jig-Guide Setting | Hole Size |
| **RIGHT REAR LEG** | | |
| A | B1 | 5/8" |
| A | B4 | 5/8" |
| A | E7 | 3/4" |
| A | G10 | 1/4" |
| A | G11 | 1/4" |
| A | G12 | 1/4" |
| A | G13 | 1/4" |
| A | G14 | 1/4" |
| A | G15 | 1/4" |
| C | C2 | 5/8" |
| C | C5 | 5/8" |
| C | F8 | 3/4" |
| **LEFT REAR LEG** | | |
| A | B1 | 5/8" |
| A | B4 | 5/8" |
| A | E7 | 3/4" |
| A | G10 thru G15 | 1/4" |
| Same Drilling Sequence as Right Rear Leg | | |
| B | C2 | 5/8" |
| B | C5 | 5/8" |
| B | F8 | 3/4" |
| **RIGHT FRONT LEG** | | |
| A | B1 | 5/8" |
| A | B4 | 5/8" |
| A | E7 | 3/4" |
| D | A3 | 5/8" |
| D | A6 | 5/8" |
| D | D9 | 3/4" |
| **LEFT FRONT LEG** | | |
| A | B1 | 5/8" |
| A | B4 | 5/8" |
| A | E7 | 3/4" |
| E | A3 | 5/8" |
| E | A6 | 5/8" |
| E | D9 | 3/4" |

follow the same procedure used above to drill the holes in the left rear leg.

**10.** Cut the front legs (B) to length (17½"). Mark a reference line

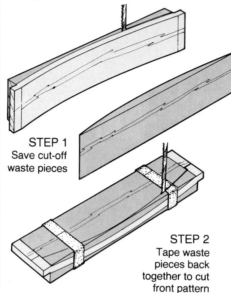

**STEP 1**
Save cut-off waste pieces

**STEP 2**
Tape waste pieces back together to cut front pattern

on one end of each leg, and use the chart to bore the holes in both legs.

**Shape the slats at the bandsaw**

**1.** From 1¼6" oak (five-quarter stock), cut the top slat (C), middle slat (D), and bottom slat (E) to the sizes listed in the Bill of Materials.

**2.** Cut a ½" rabbet ¾" deep across the ends on the back face of each slat blank. (See the Top View on the Backrest Slats drawing *below* for reference.)

**3.** Transfer the cutlines to the *top edge* of each slat blank, using the Top View for reference. (We transferred the cutlines to a piece of ¼" hardboard. Then, we cut the hardboard to shape and used it as a template to mark all the slat tops.) Bandsaw the front and back of each slat to shape as shown on Step 1 of the two-step drawing at *left*. Tape the front and back scrap pieces onto the bandsawed slat—

**BACKREST SLATS** FRONT VIEW GRID PATTERN

Each square = ½"

3/4"  5/8"

2¾"  2½"  2"  Ⓔ  Ⓓ  Ⓒ

**BACKREST SLAT** TOP VIEW GRID FOR Ⓒ, Ⓓ, AND Ⓔ

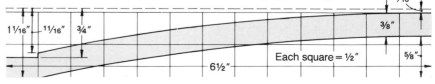

1 1/16"  1 1/16"  3/4"  1/16"  3/8"

6½"  Each square = ½"  5/8"

it's easier to mark and cut the slats with a flat front and back edge.

**4.** Using the Front View for reference, mark the cutline on the scrap front face of each slat. Now, bandsaw the top edge of each slat to shape as shown on Step 2 of the drawing *opposite*. Remove the taped on scrap pieces. (Again, we used a piece of ¼" hardboard as a template to mark the curved portion along the top of each slat.)

**5.** As shown at *right,* sand each slat to remove the saw marks.

**6.** Sand a slight round-over along the top and bottom of the tenons on each slat. (See the Chair drawing for reference.) Check the fit of the slats into their corresponding mortises in the rear chair legs. Do not glue them in place yet.

### Tenon the rails and rungs with your router

**1.** Cut the rear rail (F) and rungs (G), the front members (H, I), and the side members (J, K) to the lengths listed in the Bill of Materials from ¾" and 1" oak dowels.

**2.** Cut and shape a V-grooved block like the one shown at *right*.

**3.** Chuck a ½" straight bit into a table mounted router and position the fence where shown on Step 1 of the three-step drawing *below*. Rotate the dowel by hand to rout ⅛" into the ends of rails F, H, J. Check the fit of the tenons in their mating holes. (We practiced routing scrap dowel stock until we had the settings right.) *continued*

Sand the front and back surfaces of the backrest slats on a stationary or belt sander to remove the saw marks.

**V-GROOVE BLOCK**

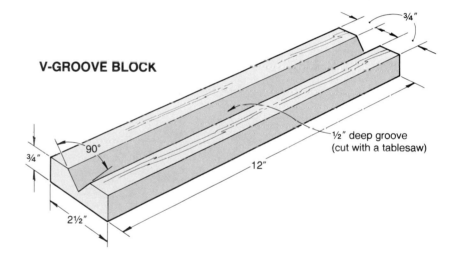

¾"

90°

¾"

2½"

½" deep groove (cut with a tablesaw)

12"

## ROUTING THE TENONS

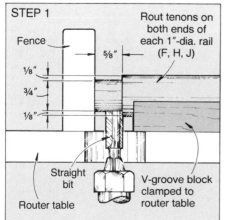

STEP 1

Fence

⅝"

⅛"

¾"

⅛"

Rout tenons on both ends of each 1"-dia. rail (F, H, J)

Straight bit

Router table

V-groove block clamped to router table

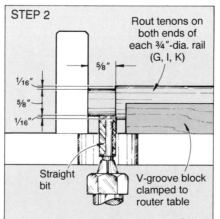

STEP 2

⅝"

1/16"

⅝"

1/16"

Rout tenons on both ends of each ¾"-dia. rail (G, I, K)

Straight bit

V-groove block clamped to router table

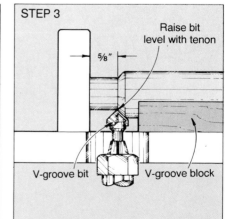

STEP 3

⅝"

Raise bit level with tenon

V-groove bit

V-groove block

# SHAKER SIMPLICITY CHAIRS
*continued*

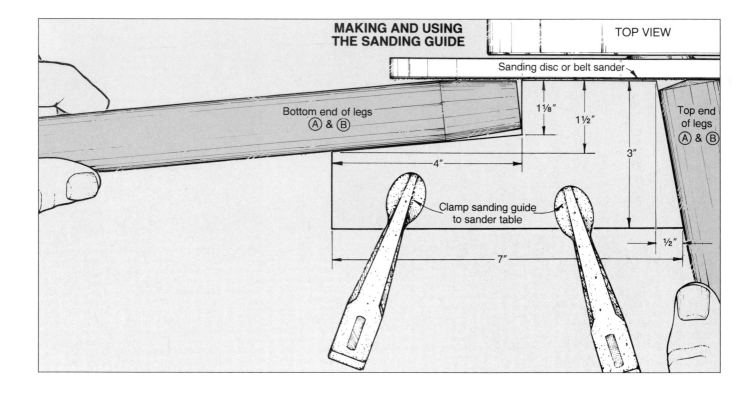

**MAKING AND USING THE SANDING GUIDE**

TOP VIEW

Sanding disc or belt sander

Bottom end of legs Ⓐ & Ⓑ

Top end of legs Ⓐ & Ⓑ

1⅛"

1½"

3"

4"

Clamp sanding guide to sander table

7"

½"

## Bill of Materials

| Part | Finished Size | | | Mat. | Qty. |
|---|---|---|---|---|---|
| | T | W | L | | |
| **SHAKER CHAIR** | | | | | |
| A rear legs | 1¼" diam. | | 38¾" | OD | 2 |
| B front legs | 1¼" diam. | | 17½" | OD | 2 |
| C top slat | 1¹⁄₁₆" | 3½" | 13" | O | 1 |
| D middle slat | 1¹⁄₁₆" | 3¼" | 13" | O | 1 |
| E bottom slat | 1¹⁄₁₆" | 2¾" | 13" | O | 1 |
| F rear rail | 1" diam. | | 13¼" | OD | 1 |
| G rear rungs | ¾" diam. | | 13¼" | OD | 2 |
| H front rail | 1" diam. | | 16¾" | OD | 1 |
| I front rungs | ¾" diam. | | 16¾" | OD | 2 |
| J side rails | 1" diam. | | 13¼" | OD | 2 |
| K side rungs | ¾" diam. | | 13¼" | OD | 4 |

**Material Key:** OD-oak dowel, O-oak

**4.** Adjust the router bit to make a ¹⁄₁₆" cut, leaving a ⅝" tenon ⅜" long on the ends of each ¾" dowel as shown on Step 2. Rout the tenons on the chair rungs (G, I, K) as you did before with the rails.

**5.** To chamfer the tenon shoulders, switch to a V-groove bit and adjust the height to rout the chamfers on the 1" dowels as shown on Step 3 of the drawing. Then, adjust the bit height for the ¾" dowels and rout their chamfers.

## How to shape the chair leg ends

**1.** Cut the sanding guide to the shape shown on the drawing *above* from 1½"-thick stock (we used a section of a 2x4). Clamp the guide to your disc-sander table (you also could use a belt sander on a stand). Using the Top-View drawing for reference, sand a 10° chamfer on the top end of each chair leg (A, B).

**2.** Sand a 1½" taper on the bottom of each chair leg where shown on the Top View drawing.

## Assemble and finish your chair

**1.** On a flat surface, glue and clamp together the chair-back assembly (A, C, D, E, F, G). (We used clamp blocks to prevent denting the oak dowels.) With a framing square, check for square and wipe off excess glue with a damp rag.

**2.** Use the same procedure to assemble the front (B, H, I).

**3.** Glue the side rails and rungs (J, K) between the front and back assemblies. (Because of the angled front and back, we used band clamps—bar clamps have a tendency to slip on the angled legs.)

**4.** Later, remove the clamps and finish-sand the chair. Apply stain and finish (we used polyurethane).

## WEAVING THE SEAT

**STEP 1.** Cut 2" radius from front corners of foam cushion. Tape cushion in place. Remove tape after completing Step 4.

**STEP 2.** Nail end of fabric tape to bottom side of top back rail. Wet cut end of tape with glue to prevent fraying.

**STEP 3.** Pull the warp over the top of the front top rail, then back around under the bottom of the rear rail. Repeat all the way across the width of the chair, keeping the warps tight.

**STEP 4.** Nail the end of the twelfth warp to the bottom of the rail.

**STEP 5.** Nail end of woof to bottom side of side rail.

**STEP 6.** Weave woof through the warps, keeping the woofs tight.

**STEP 7.** Nail end of eleventh woof to the bottom side of the side rail.

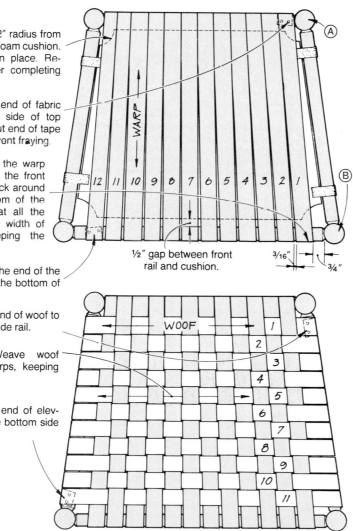

½" gap between front rail and cushion.

## Add the webbing and take a seat

*Note: The seat-weaving kit described in the Buying Guide comes complete with weaving instructions. Although you can follow their instructions, we have simplified the procedure as shown at left.*

## Buying guide

• **Oak dowels.** Three 1¼x48" oak dowels, two 1x36" oak dowels, and four ¾x36" oak dowels (enough for one chair). For the current price, contact Midwest Dowel Works, Inc., 4631 Hutchinson Road, Cincinnati, OH 45248, or call 513-574-8488 to order.

•**Seat-weaving kit.** 25 yards of 100% cotton webbing, foam cushion, tacks (enough for one chair). For a list of chair tape colors and current prices, contact Shaker Workshops, PO Box 1028, Concord, MA 01742, or call 617-646-8985.

## Project Tool List

Tablesaw
Bandsaw
Drill
Drill press
   Bits: ⁷⁄₆₄", ⁵⁄₃₂", ¼", ⅝", ¾", 1¼"
Router
   ½" straight bit
   V-groove bit
Belt sander
Disc sander
Finishing sander

*Note: We built this project using the tools listed. You may be able to substitute other tools and equipment for listed items you don't have. You'll also need various common hand tools and clamps to complete the project.*

# SHAKER-STYLE BUFFET

T hough the Shakers built their furniture with solid wood and through dovetails, they'd feel right at home with the styling of our much simplified cherry buffet. For reasons of cost, stability, and ease of construction, the cabinet carcass was designed with plywood framed in solid cherry. Also the original box-on-the-floor look was traded in for a complementary base that's compatible with many of today's decors.

## Start with the carcass

**1.** Rip and crosscut the cabinet top (A), bottom (B), end panels (C), fixed shelves (D), and divider (E) to the sizes listed in the Bill of Materials from ¼" cherry plywood. For ease in laying out and cutting, see the Cutting Diagram for our layout.

**2.** Cut or rout the rabbets and dadoes in pieces A, B, C, and E where dimensioned on the Exploded View and Part View drawings. (We used our tablesaw and a dado blade.)

**3.** Dry-clamp the pieces to check the fit; trim if necessary. Now, glue and clamp the pieces, checking for square.

**4.** Measure the opening and cut the ¼"-plywood back (F) to size.

**5.** Cut the center support (G) to size. Then, mark and cut the notch along the bottom edge where shown on the Exploded View drawing. Glue it in place directly under the divider (E).

## Now, add the face frame

**1.** From solid ¾" cherry stock, cut the bottom rail (H), stiles (I), top rail (J), mullion (K), and center rails (L) to the sizes listed in the Bill of Materials.

**2.** Dry-clamp the face frame together. Measure the length and width of the clamped-up face frame and compare to the assembled cabinet; they should be the same. The bottom of the face frame sits ¼" above the ends (C) where shown on the Side View Section drawing on the next page. Mark the dowel-hole location centerlines across each joint. See the Face Frame drawing and accompanying Dowel Hole detail for reference. Remove the clamps.

**3.** Using a doweling jig and the marked centerlines, drill ⅜" holes 11/16" deep for the dowel pins.

**4.** Glue, dowel, and clamp the frame, checking for square. Later, remove the clamps and excess glue. Sand the front and back of the face frame smooth.

**5.** Glue and clamp the face frame to the cabinet as shown in the photo *below*. *continued*

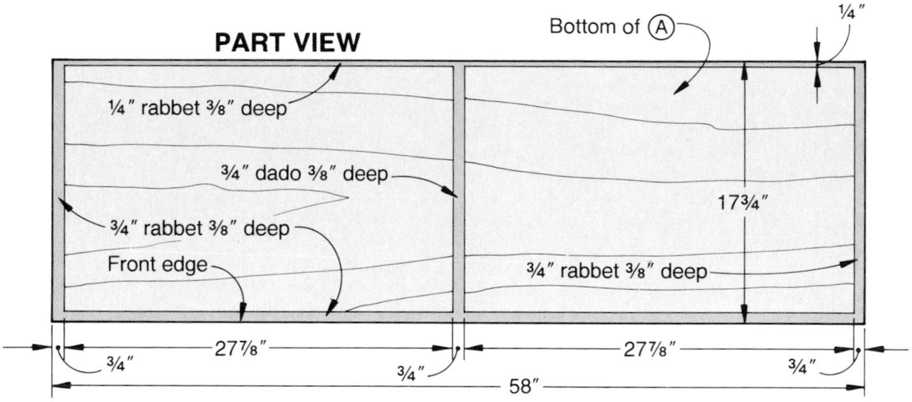
PART VIEW
Bottom of (A)
¼"
¼" rabbet ⅜" deep
¾" dado ⅜" deep
¾" rabbet ⅜" deep
Front edge
17¾"
¾" rabbet ⅜" deep
¾"
27⅞"
¾"
27⅞"
¾"
58"

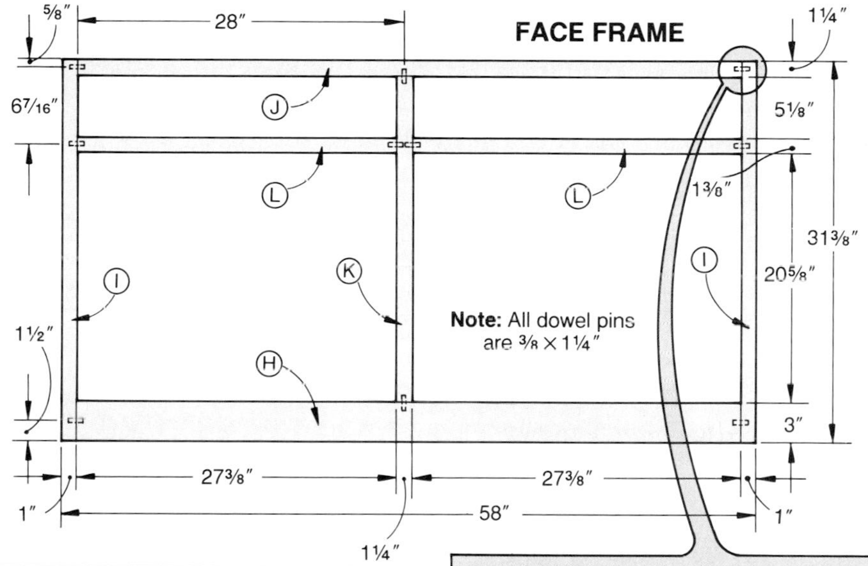
FACE FRAME
⅝"
28"
1¼"
6 7/16"
(J)
5⅛"
(L)
(L)
1⅜"
31⅜"
(I)
(K)
(I)
20⅝"
Note: All dowel pins are ⅜ X 1¼"
1½"
(H)
3"
27⅜"
27⅜"
1"
58"
1"
1¼"

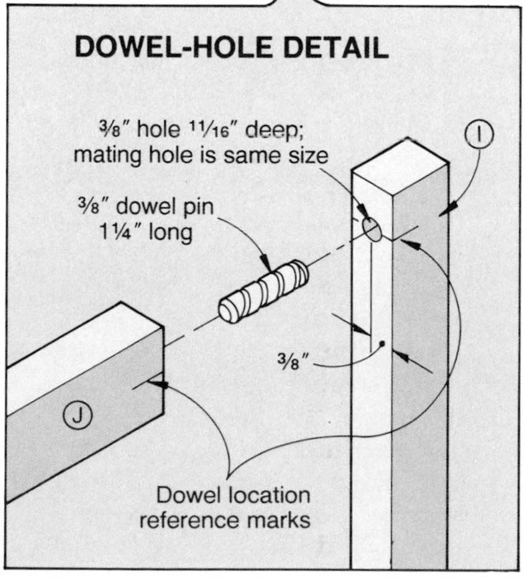
DOWEL-HOLE DETAIL
⅜" hole 11/16" deep; mating hole is same size
(I)
⅜" dowel pin 1¼" long
⅜"
(J)
Dowel location reference marks

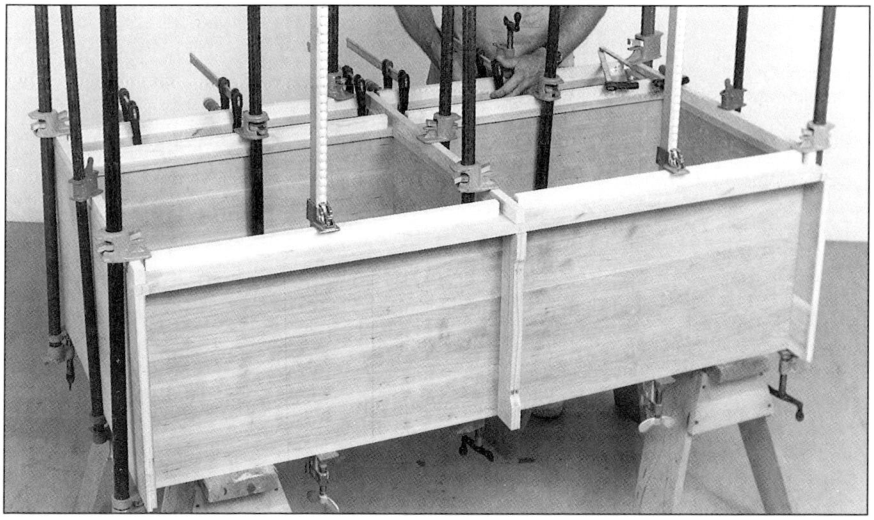

**Using over a dozen bar clamps, our project builder rests the buffet on its back while gluing and clamping the face frame to the carcass.**

# SHAKER-STYLE BUFFET

*continued*

## Apply the trim

**1.** Cut one piece of ¾" cherry to 3¼" wide by 61" long for the front trim pieces (M, O) and two pieces 3¼" wide by 20" long for the side trim pieces (N, P).

**2.** Follow the five-cut sequence shown in the drawing on page 86 to form the decorative front trim pieces (M, O) from the 61"-long piece and the side trim pieces (N, P) from the 20"-long pieces. (We tested each cut first on a piece of scrap stock.)

**3.** Miter-cut the front and side trim pieces to length. Next, mark the notch on the bottom of the front trim piece (M) using the Trim detail

accompanying the Exploded View drawing for dimensions. Cut the notch with its angled ends to shape. (We marked the notch, cut just outside the marked line with a jigsaw, and then sanded to the line.)

**4.** Glue and clamp the trim pieces to the cabinet. As shown in the Side Section drawing accompanying the Exploded View drawing, the front trim piece sits ¼" below the bottom edge of face-frame member (H) and flush with the bottom edge of the cabinet side pieces (C).

*continued*

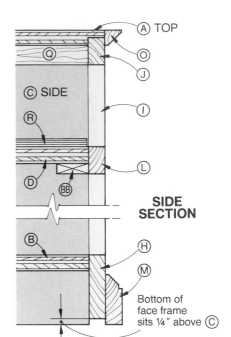

SIDE SECTION

Bottom of face frame sits ¼" above C

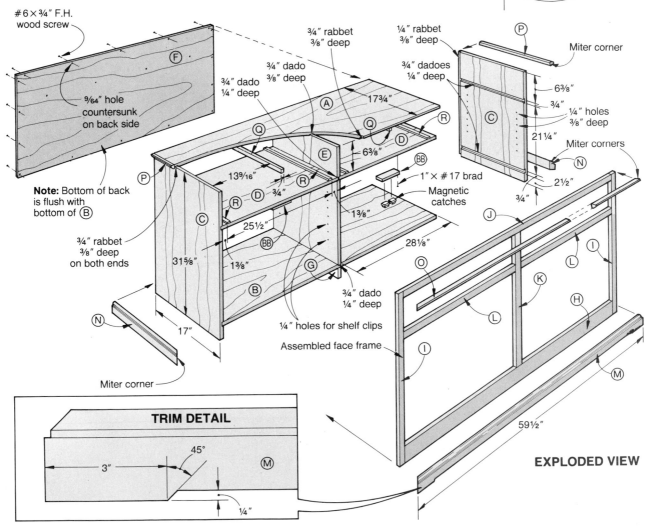

TRIM DETAIL

EXPLODED VIEW

## Bill of Materials

| Part | Finished Size* T | W | L | Mat. | Qty. |
|---|---|---|---|---|---|
| **CARCASS** | | | | | |
| A top | ¾" | 17¾" | 58" | CP | 1 |
| B bottom | ¾" | 16¾" | 57" | CP | 1 |
| C end panels | ¾" | 17" | 31⅝" | CP | 2 |
| D fixed shel | ¾" | 16¾" | 28⅜" | CP | 2 |
| E divider | ¾" | 16¾" | 28⅝" | CP | 1 |
| F back | ¼" | 29⅛" | 57¼" | CP | 1 |
| G ctr support | ¾" | 2½" | 17" | C | 1 |
| **FACE FRAME** | | | | | |
| H bottom rail | ¾" | 3" | 56" | C | 1 |
| I stiles | ¾" | 1" | 31⅜" | C | 2 |
| J top rail | ¾" | 1¼" | 56" | C | 1 |
| K mullion | ¾" | 1¼" | 27⅛" | C | 1 |
| L center rails | ¾" | 1⅜" | 27⅜" | C | 2 |
| **TRIM** | | | | | |
| M* btm frt | ¾" | 2¼" | 59½" | C | 1 |
| N* btm sides | ¾" | 2¼" | 18½" | C | 2 |
| O* top front | ¾" | ¾" | 59½" | C | 1 |
| P* top sides | ¾" | ¾" | 18½" | C | 2 |
| **DRAWERS AND GUIDES** | | | | | |
| Q kickers | ¾" | ⅞" | 16¾" | C | 2 |
| R runners | ¾" | ¼" | 16¾" | C | 4 |
| S fronts | ¾" | 5⅝" | 27⅞" | C | 2 |
| T sides | ½" | 4¾" | 17" | C | 4 |
| U backs | ½" | 4⅛" | 26⅛" | C | 2 |
| V bottoms | ¼" | 15⅞" | 26⅛" | CP | 2 |
| **DOORS** | | | | | |
| W stiles | ¾" | 2" | 21⅛" | C | 8 |
| X rails | ¾" | 2" | 10⅞" | C | 8 |
| Y* panels | ½" | 10 13/16" | 18 1/16" | EC | 4 |
| **SHELVES** | | | | | |
| Z shelves | ¾" | 15¾" | 27¾" | CP | 2 |
| AA fronts | ¾" | ⅜" | 27¾" | C | 2 |
| **MOUNTING BLOCKS** | | | | | |
| BB blocks | ⅝" | 1½" | 5" | C | 2 |

* Initially cut parts marked with an * oversized. Then, trim each to finished size according to how-to instructions.

**Material Key:** CP-cherry plywood, C-cherry, EC-edge-joined cherry

**Supplies:** #6 x ¾" flathead wood screws, ⅜" dowel pins 1¼" long, 1" x #17 brads, ⅜" inset hinges (we used Stanley 1535 semi-concealed 2" cabinet hinges; color US10A), shelf clips, magnetic catches and strike plates, finish.

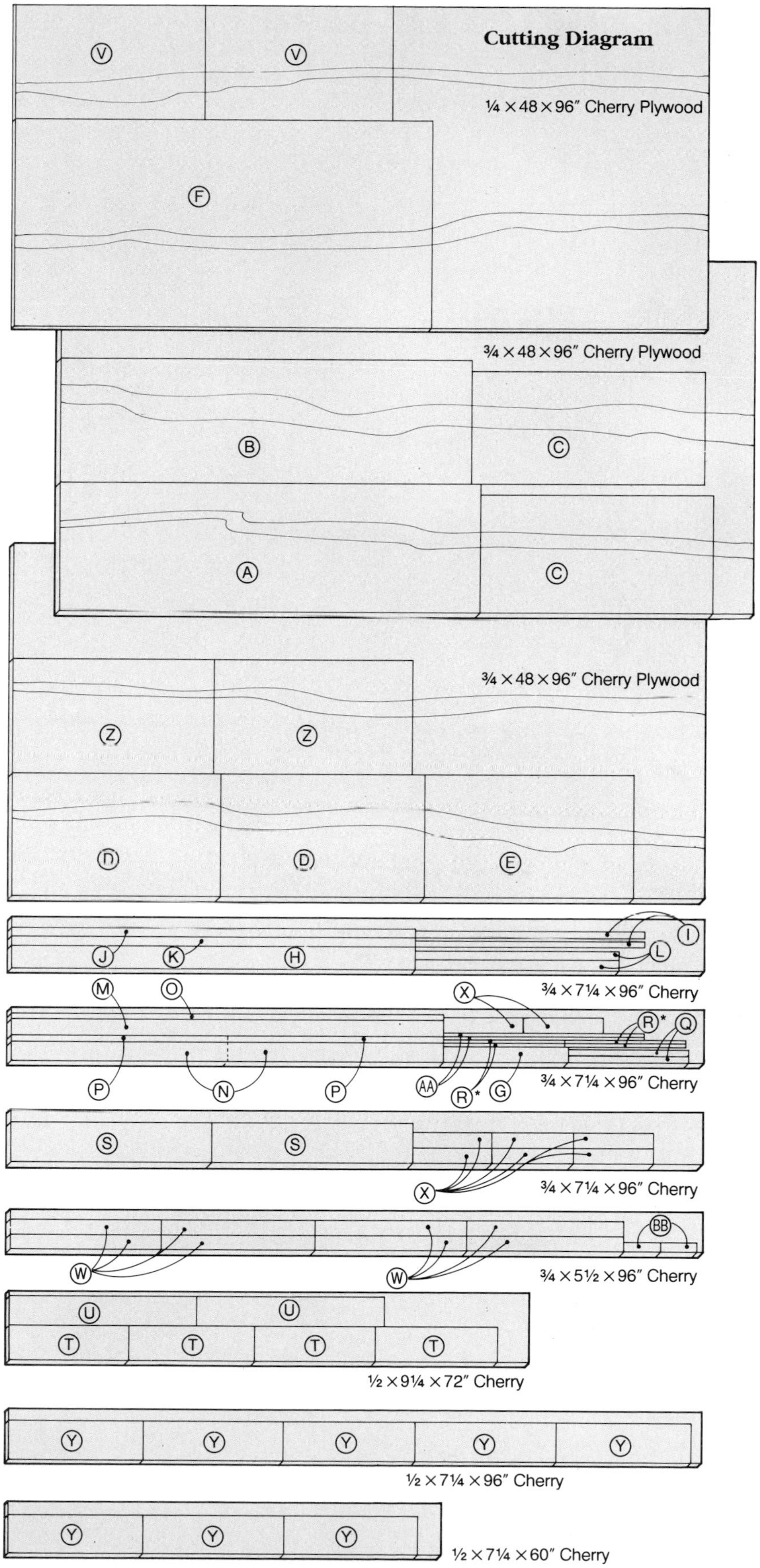

Cutting Diagram
¼ × 48 × 96" Cherry Plywood
¾ × 48 × 96" Cherry Plywood
¾ × 48 × 96" Cherry Plywood
¾ × 7¼ × 96" Cherry
¾ × 7¼ × 96" Cherry
¾ × 7¼ × 96" Cherry
¾ × 5½ × 96" Cherry
½ × 9¼ × 72" Cherry
½ × 7¼ × 96" Cherry
½ × 7¼ × 60" Cherry

# SHAKER-STYLE BUFFET

*continued*

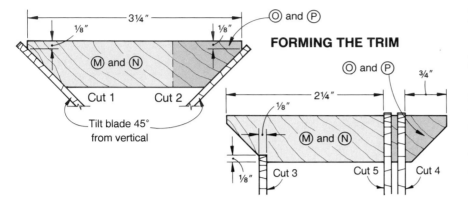

**FORMING THE TRIM**

## The guide parts and drawers come next

**1.** Cut the kickers (Q) and runners (R) to size. Glue and clamp them to the cabinet where shown on the Exploded View drawing.

**2.** Cut the two drawer fronts (S) to size from ¾" cherry. (For a continuous grain pattern across the fronts, we cut them from one board, end to end, where shown on the Cutting Diagram.)

**3.** From ½" cherry, cut the drawer sides (T) and backs (U) to size. Cut the drawer bottoms (V) to size from ¼" cherry plywood.

**4.** Cut the rabbets, grooves, and dadoes in the drawer parts where shown in the Drawer drawing.

**5.** Dry-clamp each drawer to check the fit. The bottom edge of the drawer front sits ⅜" lower than the bottom edge of the sides.

**6.** Locate the centerpoints on each drawer side, snip the head off a ½" brad, and use the brad as a bit to drill pilot holes. Glue and nail the drawers, checking for square.

**7.** Mark the centerpoints for the pulls. Drill ⅜" holes ½" deep centered on each drawer front.

## Time to construct the doors

**1.** Cut the stiles (W) and rails (X) to size. Cut or rout a ¼" groove ½" deep along one edge of each rail and stile where shown on the Tenon and Groove detail accompanying the Door drawing.

**2.** Cut a ½"-long tenon on each end of each rail.

**3.** Cut four pieces of ½" cherry to 10⅞"x18⅛" for the panels (Y). (To achieve the 10⅞" width, we edge-joined narrower stock.)

**4.** Cut ¾" rabbets ¼" deep along the front edges of each panel where shown on the drawing.

**5.** Test-fit the door pieces; the panel should be ⅟₁₆" undersized in each direction to allow it to expand. Glue and clamp the stiles, rails, and panel for each door. Allow the panel to float inside the frame *without* glue.

**6.** Cut or rout ⅜" rabbets ⅜" deep along the back outside edges of the door (except the inside edge) where shown on the Hinge detail.

## Add the shelves, hardware, and then the finish

**1.** Cut the shelves (Z) and shelf fronts (AA) to size. Glue the fronts to the shelves with the top surfaces and ends flush.

**2.** Rout a ¼" round-over along the top and bottom outside edges of each attached front where shown on the Shelf drawing on page 87.

**3.** Cut a strip of scrap stock 4" wide by 21¼" long for the hole template. (We used a piece of ¼" tempered hardboard.) Mark a centerline, and drill ¼" holes where dimensioned on the Shelf-Hole Template drawing. Now, mark a B on the bottom end; this will prevent you from inadvertently flopping it end for end.

**4.** Using the template on the inside of the cabinet, drill the ¼" shelf-clip holes ⅜" deep. See the Exploded View drawing for hole location. (We used a stop on the drill bit to prevent drilling through the cabinet sides.)

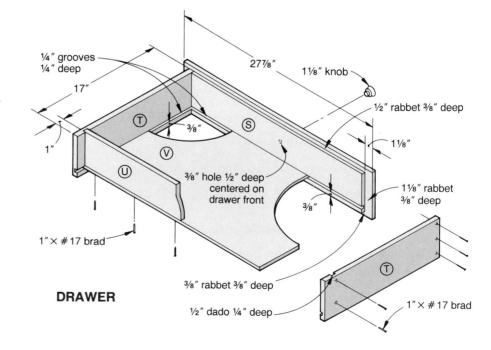

**DRAWER**

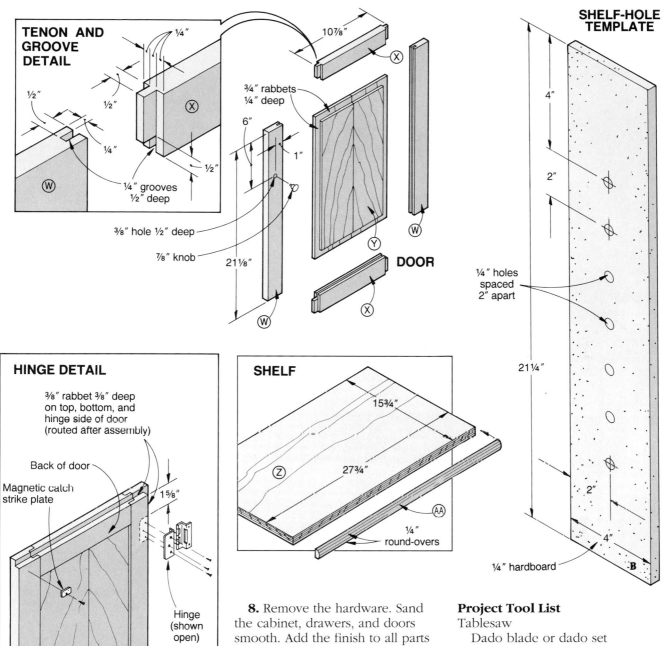

**TENON AND GROOVE DETAIL**

1/4"

1/2"

1/2"

1/4"

1/2"

1/2"

X

W

1/4" grooves 1/2" deep

3/8" hole 1/2" deep

7/8" knob

6"

1"

21 1/8"

W

10 7/8"

X

3/4" rabbets 1/4" deep

Y

W

**DOOR**

X

**SHELF-HOLE TEMPLATE**

4"

2"

1/4" holes spaced 2" apart

21 1/4"

2"

4"

1/4" hardboard

B

**HINGE DETAIL**

3/8" rabbet 3/8" deep on top, bottom, and hinge side of door (routed after assembly)

Back of door

Magnetic catch strike plate

1 5/8"

Hinge (shown open)

**SHELF**

15 3/4"

Z

27 3/4"

AA

1/4" round-overs

**5.** Add the hinges to the doors where shown on the Hinge detail. Now, with the top and bottom edges flush, and an even gap between each pair of doors, fasten the hinged doors to the cabinet.

**6.** Cut the mounting blocks (BB) to size, and glue and brad them to the bottom side of the shelves (D). Add the magnetic catches to the mounting blocks, and fasten the strikes to the door backs.

**7.** Mark the centerpoints, and drill the holes for the Shaker pull knobs in the doors.

**8.** Remove the hardware. Sand the cabinet, drawers, and doors smooth. Add the finish to all parts including the Shaker knobs, being careful not to get any finish into the holes for the knobs.

**9.** Attach the hardware, and glue the knobs in place.

**Buying Guide**
• **Cherry Shaker knobs.** Two 1 1/8" knobs and four 7/8" knobs, kit #WMB1. For the current price, contact Smith Woodworks, 101 Farmersville Road, Califon, NJ 07830, or call 908-832-2723.

**Project Tool List**
Tablesaw
    Dado blade or dado set
Router
    1/4" round-over bit
Drill
    Bits: 5/64", 9/64", 1/4", 3/8"
Finishing sander

***Note:*** *We built this project using the tools listed. You may be able to substitute other tools and equipment for listed items you don't have. You'll also need various common hand tools and clamps to complete the project.*

# EARLY-DAYS SOFA TABLE

**N**ew arrivals to America faced an enormous task in scratching out an existence in the colonies. And because they had little time or need for elaborate furniture, the pieces they crafted reflected a practical, down-home lifestyle. That straightforward design approach—as shown in the table *above*—draws raves even today from families who enjoy the country look. The table, with its single drawer, painted base, and stained top, works well behind a sofa or in a hallway.

**Start with the tapered legs**

**1.** From ¾"-thick pine stock, cut eight pieces 1⅜" wide by 30¼" long for the legs (A). With the edges and ends flush, glue and clamp together two pieces of pine, face to face, for each leg.

**2.** Scrape the excess glue from *one edge* of *each* leg, and joint or

plane the scraped edge. Using your tablesaw, rip the *opposite* edge of each leg for a 1½" finished width.

**3.** Trim *both ends* of each leg for a 29¼" finished length.

**4.** Mark the centerpoints and drill ⅜" holes ⅝" deep on two adjoining sides of each leg where located on the Leg Blank drawing on page 90. (We used a doweling jig when drilling the dowel holes.)

**5.** Using the Leg Blank drawing on page 90 for reference, locate and
*continued*

## Bill of Materials

| Part | Finished Size* T | W | L | Mat. | Qty. |
|---|---|---|---|---|---|
| **TABLE** | | | | | |
| A* legs | 1½" | 1½" | 29¼" | LP | 4 |
| B sides | ¾" | 5½" | 7" | P | 2 |
| C back | ¾" | 5½" | 32" | P | 1 |
| D front | ¾" | 5½" | 32" | EP | 1 |
| E cleats | ¾" | ¾" | 6⅞" | P | 2 |
| F drw liners | ¾" | 4½" | 7¾" | P | 2 |
| G guides | ¾" | ¾" | 7¾" | P | 4 |
| H cleats | ¾" | ¾" | 4½" | P | 4 |
| I* top | ¾" | 10½" | 36" | EP | 1 |
| **DRAWER** | | | | | |
| J sides | ½" | 2⅝" | 8⅜" | P | 2 |
| K front | ½" | 2⅝" | 14½" | P | 1 |
| L back | ½" | 2" | 14½" | P | 1 |
| M bottom | ¼" | 6⅛" | 14½" | PW | 1 |
| N face | ¾" | 3⅝" | 16" | P | 1 |

*Initially cut parts marked with an * oversized. Trim each to the finished size listed according to the how-to instructions.

**Material Key:** P-pine, LP-laminated pine, EP-edge-joined pine, PW-plywood

**Supplies:** 1" dia. knob, #8 x 1¼" oval head brass wood screw, ⅜" dowel pins 1½" long, #8 x 1" flathead wood screws, #8 x 1¼" flathead wood screws, #10 x 1¼" roundhead wood screws, #10 washers, 1" x 17 brads, double-faced (carpet) tape, finish.

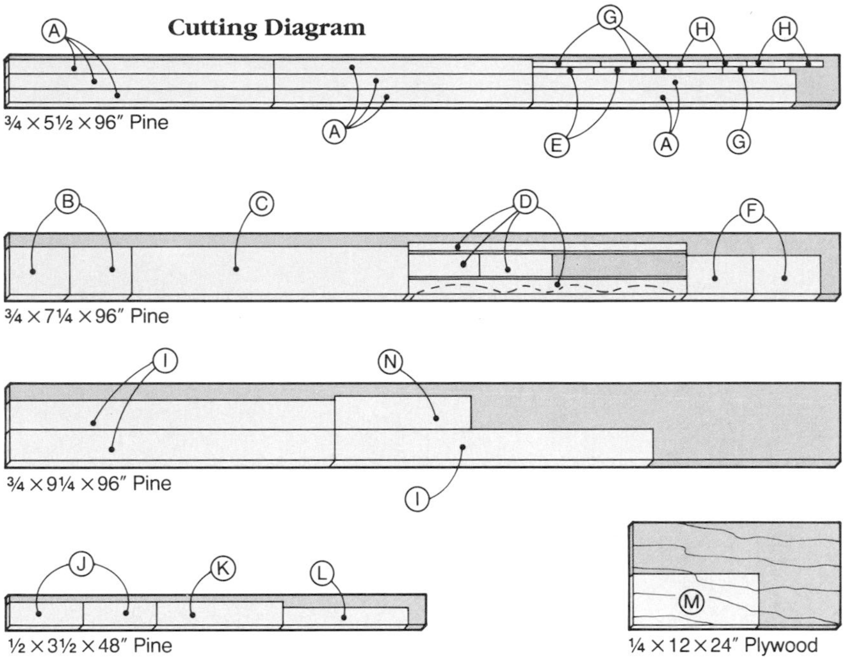

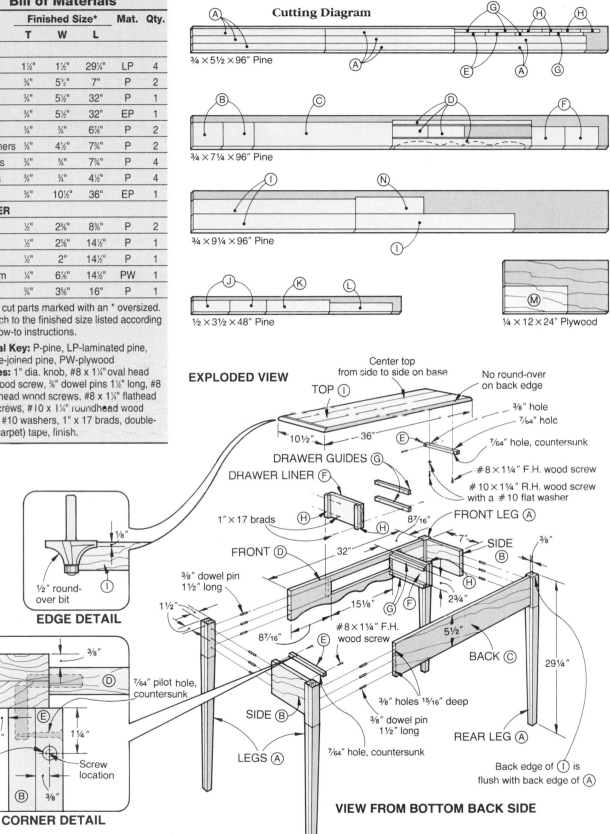

Cutting Diagram
A
G
H
H
¾ × 5½ × 96″ Pine
A
E
A
G
B
C
D
F
¾ × 7¼ × 96″ Pine
I
N
¾ × 9¼ × 96″ Pine
I
J
K
L
½ × 3½ × 48″ Pine
M
¼ × 12 × 24″ Plywood


**EXPLODED VIEW**

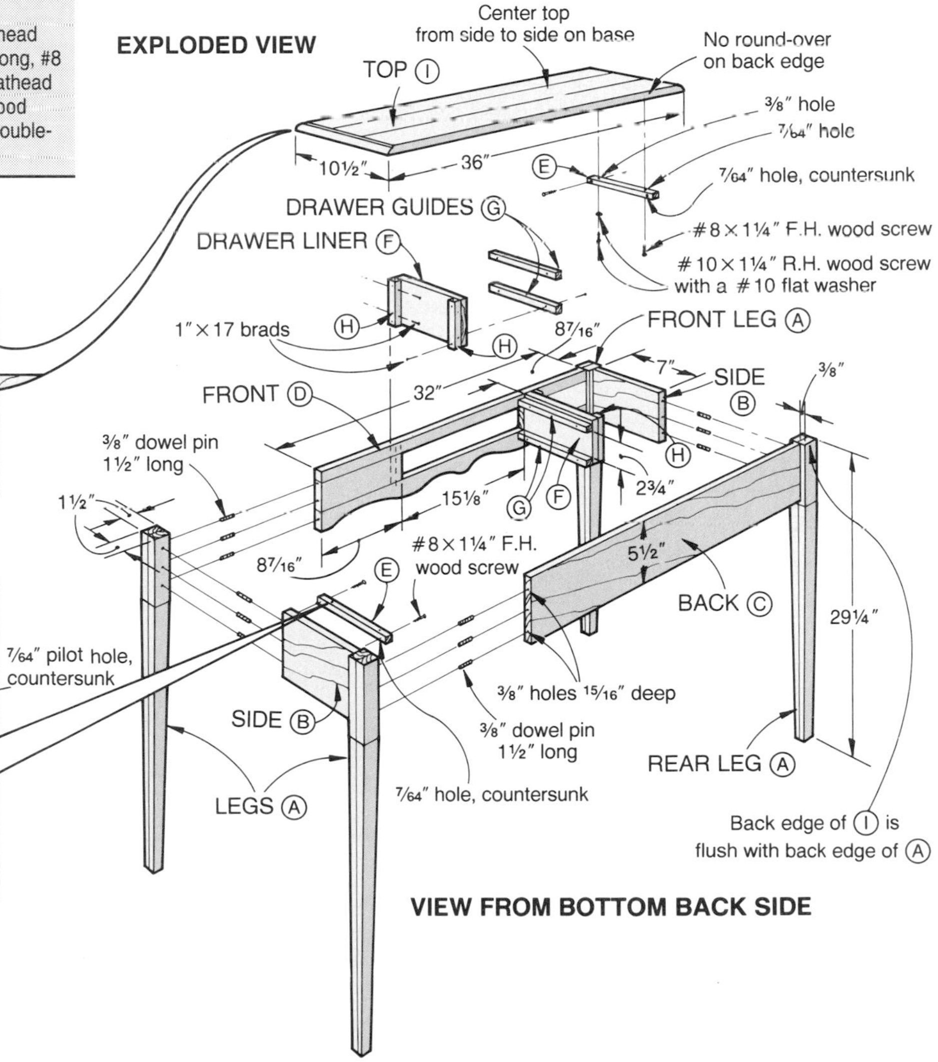

Center top from side to side on base
No round-over on back edge
TOP Ⓘ
⅜″ hole
⁷⁄₆₄″ hole
10½″
36″
Ⓔ
⁷⁄₆₄″ hole, countersunk
DRAWER GUIDES Ⓖ
DRAWER LINER Ⓕ
#8 × 1¼″ F.H. wood screw
#10 × 1¼″ R.H. wood screw with a #10 flat washer
1″ × 17 brads
Ⓗ
Ⓗ
8⁷⁄₁₆″
FRONT LEG Ⓐ
7″
SIDE Ⓑ
⅜″
FRONT Ⓓ
32″
⅜″ dowel pin 1½″ long
Ⓗ
2¾″
1½″
15⅛″
Ⓖ
Ⓕ
8⁷⁄₁₆″
#8 × 1¼″ F.H. wood screw
Ⓔ
5½″
BACK Ⓒ
29¼″
⅜″ holes ¹⁵⁄₁₆″ deep
SIDE Ⓑ
⅜″ dowel pin 1½″ long
REAR LEG Ⓐ
LEGS Ⓐ
⁷⁄₆₄″ hole, countersunk
Back edge of Ⓘ is flush with back edge of Ⓐ


**VIEW FROM BOTTOM BACK SIDE**

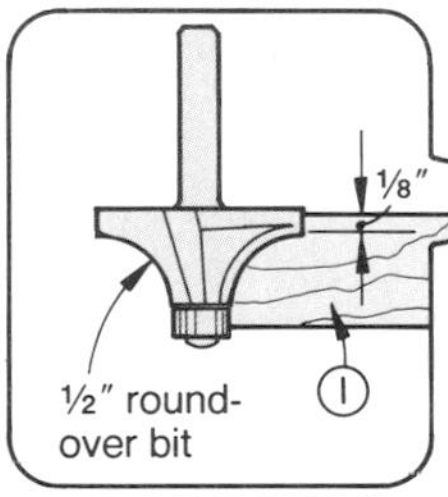

⅛″
½″ round-over bit
Ⓘ


**EDGE DETAIL**

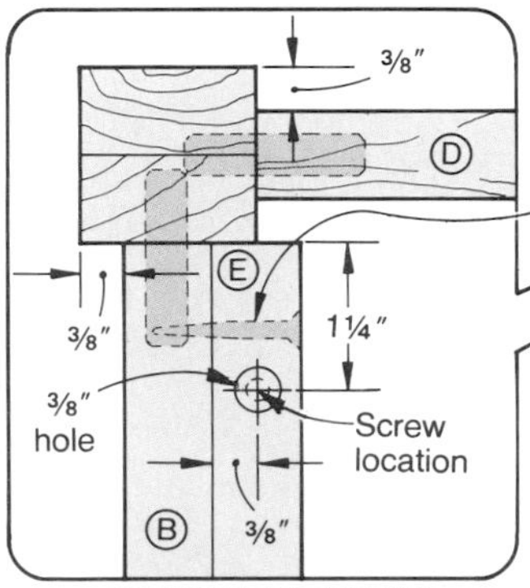

⅜″
Ⓓ
⁷⁄₆₄″ pilot hole, countersunk
Ⓔ
1¼″
⅜″
⅜″ hole
Screw location
Ⓑ
⅜″


**CORNER DETAIL**

# EARLY-DAYS SOFA TABLE
*continued*

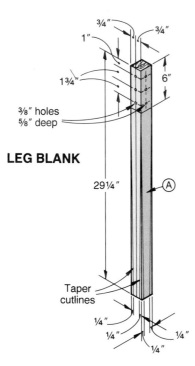

**LEG BLANK**

¾"  ¾"
1"
1¾"
⅜" holes
⅝" deep
6"
29¼"
Ⓐ

Taper
cutlines
¼"
¼"  ¼"
¼"

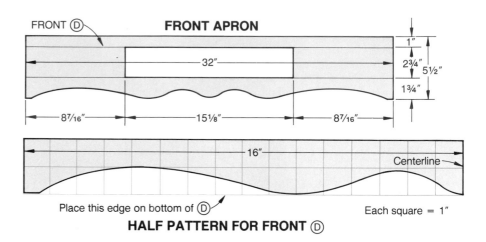

FRONT Ⓓ  **FRONT APRON**
1"
2¾"  5½"
1¾"
32"
8⁷⁄₁₆"  15⅛"  8⁷⁄₁₆"

16"  Centerline

Place this edge on bottom of Ⓓ  Each square = 1"
**HALF PATTERN FOR FRONT** Ⓓ

mark the cutlines on all four
surfaces of one leg.

**6.** Following the steps on the
drawing *below,* taper-cut each leg to
shape.

**It's time to add the aprons**
**1.** Cut the side aprons (B) and
back apron (C) to the sizes listed in
the Bill of Materials. Cut the front
apron parts (D) to the sizes shown
on the drawing *above right.*
**2.** With the ends flush, glue and
clamp together the front apron as

**Check that the ends are flush when
clamping the front-apron pieces.**

shown in the photo at *right.*
**3.** Cut a piece of heavy paper to 2
×16", and draw a 1" grid on it. Using
the grid pattern *above* for reference,

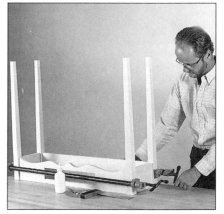

**Clamp the front apron and back
apron between the leg assemblies.**

lay out the half-pattern on the piece
of paper. To do this, mark the
points where the pattern outline
crosses each grid line. Draw lines to

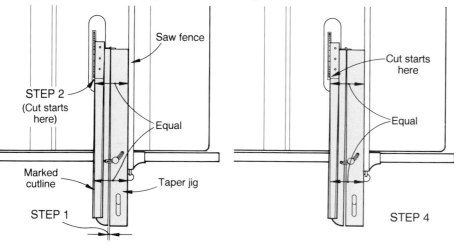

Saw fence

STEP 2
(Cut starts
here)

Equal

Marked
cutline

Taper jig

STEP 1

Cut starts
here

Equal

STEP 4

## CUTTING THE TAPERS

**STEP 1** Adjust the taper jig so
the marked cutline on the leg is
parallel to the fence.
**STEP 2** Position the fence so
blade aligns with the cutline.
**STEP 3** Cut two adjacent sides
on all four legs.
**STEP 4** Use carpet tape to adhere the scraps onto the edges
from which they were cut, so
the remaining marked cutline
is parallel with the fence. Do
not change the jig angle. Cut
two adjacent sides on each leg.

connect the points. Cut the pattern to shape, position the bottom of the template flush with the bottom of the front apron, and use it to lay out the curved bottom on one half of the apron. Repeat to mark the outline on the other half of the apron.

### Now, join the aprons to the legs

**1.** Using dowel centers, transfer the dowel-hole centerpoints from the legs to the side aprons (B), back apron (C), and front apron (D). The aprons set back ⅜" from the face of the legs where shown on the Corner detail.

**2.** Drill ⅜" holes ¹⁵⁄₁₆" deep for the dowel pins where marked in the ends of the aprons.

**3.** Glue and clamp a side apron between a front and rear leg. Using the two other legs and side apron, repeat the process.

**4.** Glue the back apron (C) and front apron (D) between the leg assemblies as photographed *opposite*. Check for square.

**5.** Cut the cleats (E) to size. Drill the mounting holes. (As shown in the Corner detail accompanying the Exploded View drawing, we drilled one of the top mounting holes oversized. This allows the mounting screw to move slightly as the top expands and contracts.) Glue and screw the cleats to the inside edge of the side aprons.

### Next, install the drawer guides

**1.** To verify the length, measure the distance between the front and back aprons. Cut the drawer liners (F) and guides (G) to the sizes listed in the Bill of Materials and to the measured length.

**2.** Glue and nail the guides flush with the top and bottom edges of the drawer opening where shown on the Exploded View drawing.

**3.** Cut the mounting cleats (H) to size, and glue and nail them to the outside surface of each drawer liner flush with the ends.

**4.** Glue and nail the drawer-guide assemblies (F, G, H) between the front and back aprons. The inside edge of the drawer liners (F) should be flush with the inside edge of the drawer opening in the front apron.

### And now for the tabletop

**1.** Cut three pieces of ¾" pine stock to 37" long by 3½" wide for the top panel (I). Edge-join the pieces with the surfaces and ends flush. Use clamp blocks to prevent denting the pine edges.

**2.** Scrape the excess glue and sand smooth. Trim the top panel to 36" long. Rout a ½" round-over bit along the front and side edges of the tabletop. See the Edge detail accompanying the Exploded View drawing for reference.

### Add the drawer for a bit of storage

**1.** Rip and crosscut the drawer sides (J), front (K), back (L), and bottom (M) to the sizes listed in the Bill of Materials.

**2.** Cut a ¼" groove ¼" deep, ⅜" from the bottom edge of the drawer sides and drawer front. (See the Drawer drawing *below* for reference.) Now, cut a ½" dado ¼" deep, 2" from the back end of each drawer side. Also, cut a ½" rabbet ¼" deep along the front inside edge of each drawer side.

**3.** Drill and countersink a pair of ⁵⁄₃₂" holes through the drawer front (K) where shown on the Drawer drawing. You'll use these holes to attach the drawer face (N) to the drawer front later.

**4.** Dry-clamp the drawer pieces to check the fit of the pieces and to check the fit of the drawer into the front-apron opening. Glue and clamp the drawer together, checking for square. Do not glue the bottom (M) in the ¼" groove; instead, secure it to the back (L) with 1"x17 brads. (We butted masking tape on the inside of each drawer corner to catch excess glue. After the glue dried, we peeled off the tape. This saves lots of sanding and prevents unsightly chisel or scraper marks that result from trying to remove the hardened glue from the soft pine.)

**5.** Cut the drawer face (N) to size. Drill a ⅛" hole in the center of the face for attaching the knob.

**6.** Rout a ⅜" round-over along the front edges of the drawer face.

**7.** Screw the drawer face (N) to the drawer front (K).

### Sand smooth and add the country finish

**1.** Sand smooth the base, tabletop, and drawer.

**2.** Finish as desired. For information on how to achieve the country look like that on the sofa-table base, refer to the country-finish techniques described in the Candle Box project on page 60. (For the sofa table and other pieces in this section and elsewhere, here are the finishes in the order we applied them: Wood Kote's traditional walnut stain, clear *continued*

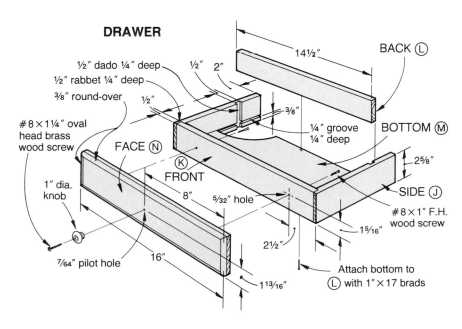

**DRAWER**

½" dado ¼" deep
½" rabbet ¼" deep
⅜" round-over
#8 × 1¼" oval head brass wood screw
FACE (N)
1" dia. knob
⁷⁄₆₄" pilot hole
½" 2"
½"
14½"
BACK (L)
⅜"
¼" groove ¼" deep
BOTTOM (M)
(K)
FRONT
8"
⁵⁄₃₂" hole
2½"
16"
1¹³⁄₁₆"
2⅝"
SIDE (J)
#8 × 1" F.H. wood screw
1⁵⁄₁₆"
Attach bottom to (L) with 1" × 17 brads

# EARLY-DAYS SOFA TABLE

*continued*

lacquer, Sherwin-Williams cajun red paint, Stubb's soldier blue paint, Bartley's jet mahogany gel stain, and two coats of satin polyurethane.)

**3.** Stain the tabletop and apply the finish following the instructions for the way we "aged" the wood on a small stool. (We used Wood Kote's traditional walnut stain. After that dried, we used a toothbrush to splatter on Bartley's jet mahogany gel stain, followed by two coats of clear satin polyurethane.)

**4.** When dry, place the tabletop (I) upside down on a blanket on your workbench. Position the table base, also upside down, on the tabletop. With the back edges flush, center the base from side to side. Screw the base to the top through the mounting cleats (E) where shown on the Exploded View drawing. Insert the #10x1¼" roundhead wood screws with washers through the ⅜" holes and drive tight. Then, loosen the screw one full turn to allow for seasonal expansions and contractions of the tabletop.

**5.** Add a 1" knob to the drawer. (We used a porcelain knob— available at most hardware stores—and attached it with a #8x1¼" oval head brass wood screw. To prevent the screw from working loose, we added a drop of epoxy to the threads.)

### Project Tool List
Tablesaw
   Dado blade or dado set
Bandsaw
Jointer
Drill
   Bits: ⁷⁄₆₄", ⅛", ⁵⁄₃₂", ⅜"
Router
   ⅜" round-over bit
   ½" round-over bit
Finishing sander

**Note:** *We built this project using the tools listed. You may be able to substitute other tools and equipment for listed items you don't have. You'll also need various common hand tools and clamps to complete the project.*

## Creating a natural wood finish

To make a natural wood surface look old, as we did with the top on the sofa table, follow these steps:

**1.** Distress the piece just as described in the Candle Box project on page 60, keeping in mind that the surface will look older and older with every scratch, nick, and dent.

**2.** Apply a dark stain to areas such as the base of legs and other places along edges where dirt would likely accumulate over time as shown at right. Add the same stain to scratches and nicks to accentuate these blemishes. Again, we prefer gel stains for greater controllability.

**3.** Apply a lighter stain to the remaining areas, and blend the stains where they meet. Let both stains sit for a few minutes, then wipe away the excess.

**4.** Lighten heavily worn areas with paint thinner before the stain dries. As shown at right, we lightened the areas of the foot stool where shoes would have likely worn off the finish. To add highlights along edges and corners, sand lightly with 320-grit paper. Now, you can add spatters and a clear coat of your choice.

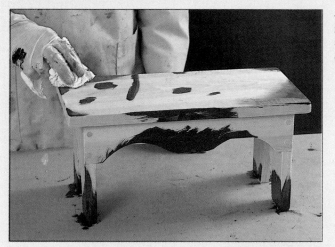

**Apply a dark gel stain to areas prone to dirt buildup.**

**Before the stain dries, lighten any high-wear areas with paint thinner.**

# COMFY COUNTRY BENCH

**An** investment of less than $40 in materials and a couple of evenings in the workshop will yield a high return when building this simple, but pleasing bench. Use it indoors for informal seating or place it at garden side this summer for a comfortable seat to view the fruits of your labor.

**Note:** *We hand-picked spruce 2x12s for the ends and 2x8s for the seat and back. Pine or fir will also work well. If you have trouble locating straight and uncupped stock, edge-join narrower pieces to width. Use Titebond II, epoxy, or resorcinol for gluing outdoor projects.*

## Build the bench ends

**1.** Cut the end pieces (A) to 28¾" length from 2x12 stock. Draw a 1" grid measuring 5x10" on heavy paper or thin cardboard. Using the Heart Grid Half Pattern for reference, lay out the pattern for half a heart. Cut the template to shape.

**2.** Position the template, and trace the heart outline 3" from the top of each end piece where located on the End View drawing. Cut the outlines to shape on the bandsaw or with a jigsaw, and drum-sand to remove the saw marks.

**3.** To join the end pieces, start by clamping each pair of 2x12s (A) together edge to edge, with the top and bottom edges flush. Now, using the dimensions on the Exploded View drawing, mark the three dowel hole locations on one face. Remove the clamps. Using a square, transfer the lines to the inside edge of each end piece.

**4.** Check that you're square to the surface, and drill ¾" holes 1½" deep centered from edge to edge where marked. (We used a portable electric drill.)

**5.** From ¾" dowel stock, set a stop, and cut six pieces 3⅜" long. Sand a chamfer on each end. (We formed our chamfers on a belt sander.)

**6.** Next, cut four ⅜"-thick scrap spacers. Glue, dowel, and clamp both bench ends together, placing the ⅜" spacers between the end pieces for a consistent ⅜" gap as shown on page 94. Save the spacers—you'll use them when joining the seat and back pieces later. *continued*

# COMFY COUNTRY BENCH
*continued*

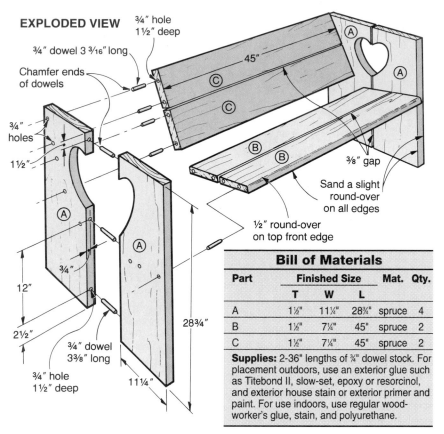

**EXPLODED VIEW**

¾" hole 1½" deep

¾" dowel 3 ³⁄₁₆" long

Chamfer ends of dowels

45"

¾" holes

1½"

¾"

12"

2½"

¾" dowel 3⅜" long

¾" hole 1½" deep

28¾"

11¼"

³⁄₈" gap

Sand a slight round-over on all edges

½" round-over on top front edge

| Bill of Materials | | | | |
|---|---|---|---|---|
| Part | Finished Size | | Mat. | Qty. |
| | T | W | L | | |
| A | 1½" | 11¼" | 28¾" | spruce | 4 |
| B | 1½" | 7¼" | 45" | spruce | 2 |
| C | 1½" | 7¼" | 45" | spruce | 2 |

**Supplies:** 2-36" lengths of ¾" dowel stock. For placement outdoors, use an exterior glue such as Titebond II, slow-set, epoxy or resorcinol, and exterior house stain or exterior primer and paint. For use indoors, use regular woodworker's glue, stain, and polyurethane.

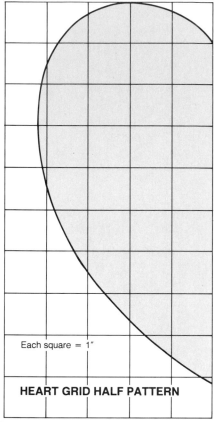

Each square = 1"

**HEART GRID HALF PATTERN**

**7.** Sand a slight round-over on all edges of each bench end.

**8.** From 2×8" stock, cut the two seat pieces (B) and backrest pieces (C) to length.

**9.** Select one seat piece for the front, and rout a ½" round-over on the top front edge.

### Mark and drill all the dowel holes

**1.** Mark a pair of intersecting lines for locating the dowel-hole center points on the *outside face* of each bench end, using the dimensions on the End View drawing.

**2.** Locate and mark the eight dowel-hole centerpoints on the lines on each bench end.

**3.** Bore ¾" holes through the bench ends at the marked centerpoints, backing the stock with scrap to prevent chip-out. (We clamped a piece of 2×4 on the inside face

before drilling the first holes. Then, we repositioned the 2×4 and drilled the other four holes.)

### Assemble the pieces

**1.** From ¾"-diameter dowel stock, set a stop, and cut 16 dowels 3³⁄₁₆" long. Sand a ³⁄₁₆" chamfer on both ends of each dowel.

**2.** Cut four 1×2 scraps to 26" long. Clamp two strips to the inside face of each bench end where shown on the drawing at *right*. The strips help center the seat and backrest pieces over the ¾" holes for drilling in the next step. (We positioned a piece of scrap 2×8 stock on each strip to check that the holes would center in the end of the stock.)

**3.** With a helper, position the seat pieces where located on the End View drawing. Slip the ³⁄₈" spacers between the pieces for a consistent gap. Then, clamp the seat pieces

firmly between the bench ends, as shown in the photo *opposite*.

**4.** Chuck a ¾" bit into a portable electric drill. Using the previously drilled holes in the end sections as guides, drill a pair of 1½"-deep holes squarely into each seat piece as shown in the photo *opposite*. As

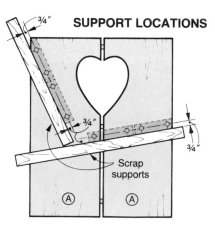

**SUPPORT LOCATIONS**

¾"

¾"

¾"

Scrap supports

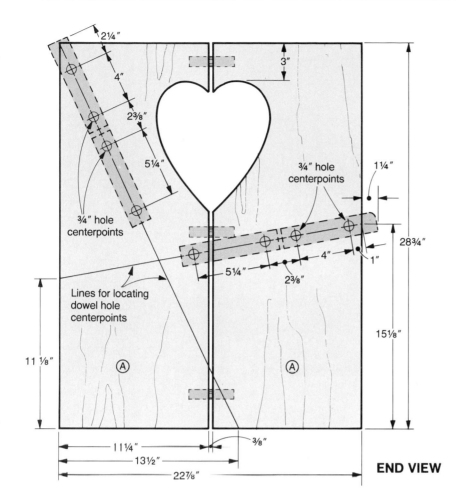

2¼"
4"
2³⁄₈"
5¼"

¾" hole
centerpoints

¾" hole
centerpoints

Lines for locating
dowel hole
centerpoints

11 ⅛"

Ⓐ

3"

¾" hole
centerpoints

1¼"

28¾"

Ⓐ

15⅛"

5¼"
2³⁄₈"
4"
1"

11¼"
13½"
22⅞"
3⁄₈"

**END VIEW**

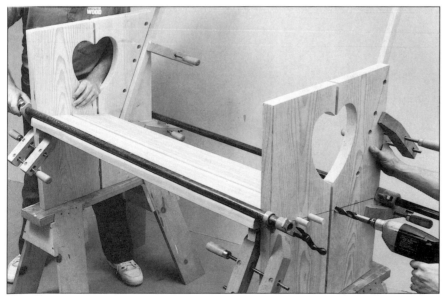

**Position the two seat and two back pieces on the support strips, and clamp them in place between the end pieces. Then, use the previously drilled ¾" holes in the bench ends as guides, and drill dowel holes 1½" deep into the seat pieces.**

soon as you've drilled the first hole, insert one of the 3³⁄₁₆"-long dowels into the hole to help steady the seat piece for drilling the next hole. Do not insert the dowel more than ½" into the seat piece; you may have trouble removing it if you do.

**5.** Repeat the procedure to drill the ¾" holes in both ends of the backrest pieces.

**6.** Remove one of the 3³⁄₁₆"-long dowels. With a small brush, coat the inside of the hole with glue. To prevent marring the chamfered dowel end, use a rubber-tipped mallet to slowly drive the dowel into the hole. Drive the dowel until just the chamfered end protrudes. Be careful not to drive the dowels too far—they're almost impossible to back out. Immediately wipe off any excess glue with a damp cloth. Repeat for each remaining dowel. Let the glue dry and then remove the clamps.

### Sand, paint and enjoy

**1.** Sand the entire bench, sanding a slight round-over on all edges.

**2.** To keep the wood grain visible, finish the bench with an exterior house stain for use outdoors. For use indoors, apply regular stain and a clear finish such as polyurethane. If you wish to paint the bench and set it outside, apply an exterior primer followed by two coats of exterior paint. Use an interior primer and paint for use indoors.

### Project Tool List
Tablesaw
Bandsaw
Drill
   Bit: ¾"
Drum sander
Belt sander
Router
   ½" round-over bit
Finishing sander

*Note:* We built this project using the tools listed. You may be able to substitute other tools and equipment for listed items you don't have. You'll also need various common hand tools and clamps to complete the project.

# ACKNOWLEDGMENTS

## Project Designers

David Ashe—Oak Breakfast Tray, pages 9–11; Kitchen Canisters and Brass Scoop, pages 12–15; Spice Cabinet, pages 16–20; Paper Towel Holder, pages 21–23; Country-Colors Quilt Stand, pages 56–57

Timothy Burke—Prizewinning Plate Rack, pages 35–36

James R. Downing—Country-Kitchen Butter Churn, pages 5–8; Folding Muffin Stand, pages 24–27; The Organized Cook's Companion, pages 28–31; Odds 'N' Ends Country Shadow Box, pages 48–50; Simply Stated Shaker Wall Clock, pages 51–55; Trestle Table, pages 69–72; Shaker Simplicity Chairs, pages 73–81; Shaker-Style Buffet, pages 82–87; Comfy Country Bench, pages 93–95

Kim Downing—Early-American Ladder Shelf, pages 40–43

Gray Fisher—Early-Days Sofa Table, pages 88–92

Woodworkers Unlimited—Country Goose Napkin Holder, pages 32–33

Dean Young—Cherry Wall Cabinet, pages 37–39

## Photographers

Craig Anderson
Bob Calmer
John Hetherington
Hopkins Associates
Jim Kascoutas

## Illustrators

Jamie Downing
Kim Downing
Randall Foshee
Mike Henry
Jim Stevenson
Perry Struse
Bill Zaun

---

If you would like to order any additional copies of our books, call 1-800-678-2802 or check with your local bookstore.

---